W9-CHV-145

THE *Missing* SHOP MANUAL

ROUTER

THE *Missing* **SHOP MANUAL**

ROUTER

{ the tool information you need at your fingertips }

Distributed By
Fox Chapel Publishing

Fox Chapel
PUBLISHING

© 2010 by Skills Institute Press LLC
"Missing Shop Manual" series trademark of Skills Institute Press
Published and distributed in North America
by Fox Chapel Publishing Company, Inc.

Router is an original work, first published in 2010.

Portions of text and art previously published by and reproduced under license
with Direct Holdings Americas Inc.

ISBN 978-1-56523-489-5

Library of Congress Cataloging-in-Publication Data

Router.
    p. cm. -- (The missing shop manual)
  Includes index.
  ISBN 978-1-56523-489-5
  1. Routers (Tools) 2. Routing-machines. I. Fox Chapel Publishing.
  TT203.5.R665 2010
  684'.083--dc22
                              2010013438

To learn more about the other great books from Fox Chapel Publishing,
or to find a retailer near you, call toll-free 800-457-9112 or visit us at
www.FoxChapelPublishing.com.

Note to Authors: We are always looking for talented authors to write new books
in our area of woodworking, design, and related crafts. Please send a brief letter
describing your idea to Acquisition Editor, 1970 Broad Street, East Petersburg, PA
17520.

Printed in China
First printing: July 2010

WHAT YOU WILL LEARN

Chapter 1
Router Basics, page 10

Chapter 2
Edge Forming, page 54

Chapter 3
Grooving, page 92

Chapter 4
Router Joinery, page 132

Chapter 5
Freehand Routing, page 192

Designing and inventing router jigs and fixtures is somewhat of a passion of mine. Over the years I've made numerous devices—many very crude—to simplify, speed up, or facilitate seemingly impossible routing tasks. These jigs have made my cabinetmaking, relief carving, sign work, and just about every other area of wood cutting much easier and more economical. If you took away my router and my special jigs and fixtures, I would be almost helpless in the workshop.

Jig-making can be easy or complex, simple or refined. The need dictates what you build and how you build it. A few years ago I made a simple but very effective router table and fence with a couple of dollars' worth of material. Just recently, I invested $33 constructing a new router table capable of duplicating the cutting action and operations offered only by a $1500 production routing machine.

Many features of new routers, such as speed choices and easy depth-of-cut controls, can be exploited for better and safer jig-making. Plunging capability is great for some jigs, but for many I still prefer to use the motor unit without the base. Both types can be built into router tables. I've also mounted router motors horizontally on movable sleds with a template follower to make duplicate turnings. You can also mount

Patrick Spielman, a consultant and author of more than 40 woodworking books, taught professionally for three decades.

a router at various angles to the work table. This system allows you to create a variety of profiles from just one bit. For example, a round nose can be used to raise panels and cut European-style finger pull stock for doors and drawers.

Designing jigs gets easier the more often you do it. An idea that inspires one jig will invariably resurface in some form to help solve a different problem. Before building a jig, I visualize the bit making the desired cut. Then I figure out how to attach the router to the jig and move one or the other to make the cut. With more complex jigs, I need to put together one or more mock-ups before constructing the first working model. I make good use of large hose clamps and bandsawn cradles, or V clamping blocks, to hold routers.

I've made scores of jigs to simplify fairly routine woodworking jobs like spacing dadoes, cutting mortises and tenons, making various miters, and scarfing joints; I've even used the plunge router to cut dowel holes. Still, there are a lot of ideas I haven't yet tested, and a lot of jobs that can be made better and easier with just the right jig.

- Patrick Spielman

CHAPTER 1:

Router Basics

Since its invention during the First World War, the portable electric router has made its presence felt in every aspect of woodworking. It is easy to see why: The router can cut rabbets, trim laminate, bevel edges, shape molding, and make dovetail joints. It can even surface small pieces of stock and follow a pre-cut template to cut intricate patterns. The sheer number of tasks it performs easily ranks the router with any other portable or stationary woodworking tool. It is as close to a universal tool as woodworking has.

The router is a direct descendant of the hand-powered molding plane, which featured interchangeable cutters used for grooving, edge forming, and joinery. It features a motor that spins a bit at a very high speed. Just as the molding plane drew on a range of

Keeping a router from wobbling as it is fed along the edge of a workpiece to cut a profile into the face can be a tricky operation. A support board clamped to the stock can help keep the tool steady.

A non-piloted bit carves a rabbet in the edge of a board. Riding the router base plate along an edge guide produces a uniform width of cut.

standard and exotic cutters, the router can use a myriad number of interchangeable bits to create dozens of distinctive profiles, everything from chamfering cutters to beading bits *(page 16)*.

Shaping the edge of a workpiece with a decorative profile is probably the task the router is most commonly called upon to perform. There are two ways of making the cut, depending on the type of bit used. A piloted bit features a pilot bearing that rides along the edge of the work, keeping penetration of the cutter constant. With a non-piloted bit, cutting width is controlled by guiding the router along an edge guide clamped to the work.

The manner in which you cut a dado or groove depends on the type of router. A standard tool must be held above the surface of the workpiece before the motor is switched on. The entire tool is then lowered, plunging the bit into the wood. With a plunge router, the base plate can remain flat on the surface as the router is turned on and the bit is lowered into the work.

Any router can be mounted in a specially designed table that transforms it into a stationary tool, freeing your hands to feed stock into the bit. You can also install bits in a table-mounted router that cannot be used if the tool is handheld.

CHOOSING A ROUTER

Although the fixed-base router has been available for most of this century, the plunge router is a more recent invention, dating back only 30 years. But its popularity has grown exponentially in the past decade.

Each type of router has its strengths. For hand-held routing, a fixed-base tool, like the one shown on page 14 is a good choice. Fixed-base models are lighter, adjust more simply, and are generally less expensive than plunge routers of comparable size and power. Fixed-base routers work well with a router table; in most cases, separating the motor barrel from the base plate can be accomplished by loosening a screw and twisting.

For plowing grooves and mortises, a plunge router, like the model illustrated on page 15 is a good option. This type of router allows you to plunge the bit into the stock to a predetermined depth with the sub-base flat on the surface. With a fixed-base router, the tool must be held with the bit clear of the stock, turned on, and then pivoted into the surface.

Either type of router performs well in edge-forming operations. When considering a router, the tool should have variable speed; bits should be easy to change; the sub-base should be perfectly flat; the on/off switch should be easy to operate with both hands on the tool; and the router should be substantial and durable.

If you are choosing a plunge model, check for a smooth plunge action and a plunge lock that is comfortable to engage while operating the tool. Well-designed models should allow you to make minute adjustments to the plunge depth with little fuss.

ANATOMY OF A ROUTER

Standard Router

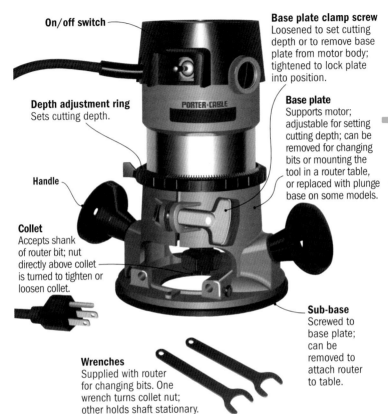

On/off switch

Base plate clamp screw
Loosened to set cutting depth or to remove base plate from motor body; tightened to lock plate into position.

Depth adjustment ring
Sets cutting depth.

Base plate
Supports motor; adjustable for setting cutting depth; can be removed for changing bits or mounting the tool in a router table, or replaced with plunge base on some models.

Handle

Collet
Accepts shank of router bit; nut directly above collet is turned to tighten or loosen collet.

Sub-base
Screwed to base plate; can be removed to attach router to table.

Wrenches
Supplied with router for changing bits. One wrench turns collet nut; other holds shaft stationary.

PORTER·CABLE

ANATOMY OF A ROUTER *(continued)*

Fixed-base Router

Anatomy of a Router

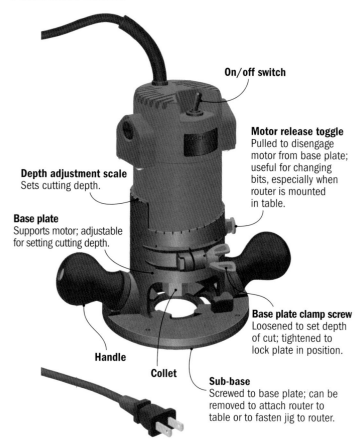

On/off switch

Motor release toggle
Pulled to disengage
motor from base plate;
useful for changing
bits, especially when
router is mounted
in table.

Depth adjustment scale
Sets cutting depth.

Base plate
Supports motor; adjustable
for setting cutting depth.

Base plate clamp screw
Loosened to set depth
of cut; tightened to
lock plate in position.

Handle

Collet

Sub-base
Screwed to base plate; can be
removed to attach router to
table or to fasten jig to router.

ANATOMY OF A ROUTER *(continued)*

Plunge Router

Front view

Depth stop bar
Sets cutting depth; gap between bar and stop screw equal depth of travel.

Micro-adjust height stop
Provides fine adjustment of cutting depth.

Plunge lock lever
Unlocked to plunge bit; locked in place when cutting depth is reached.

Variable speed dial

Handle

Height stop wheel
Limits upward plunge of motor.

Lock collet
Depressed to hold collet steady when installing or removing bit.

Base plate

Depth stop bar clamp
Loosened to release depth stop bar; tightened to set cutting depth.

Depth scale
Indicates cutting depth.

Sub-base

Stop screw
Height is adjustable to vary cutting depth of successive passes.

On/off switch

Turret stop
Rotates to position appropriate stop screw under depth stop bar.

Rear view

Collet
Holds shank of router bit; nut directly above collet is turned to tighten or loosen collet.

BITS

A typical router bit consists of a steel body with one or more cutting edges and a shank that fits into the router's collet. Most bits are made from either high-speed steel (HSS) or high-speed steel with carbide cutting edges. Although HSS bits are adequate for cutting softwood, they will not stand up to repeated use in dense hardwood. Carbide-tipped bits, while more expensive and prone

Many decorative molding bits are too big to be used safely in a hand-held router. But with the tool mounted in a router table, these large bits can transform a ½-inch router into a mini-shaper.

to chipping, stay sharp longer and cut more easily through harder wood.

Router bits can be divided into three groups according to their size and function. Edge-forming bits *(page 18)* rout decorative profiles in the edges of a workpiece or cut one or both halves of an interlocking joint. As their name implies, grooving bits *(page 20)* are designed to cut grooves and dadoes, and work best in a plunge router. The bits shown on page 22 are larger than standard bits and should be used with the router mounted in a router table.

ROUTER BITS

A router is only as good as the bit it turns.

Many experts argue that machined bits are better made than cast router bits, and double-fluted bits cut more smoothly than single-fluted cutters. Quality is, of course, important. Before buying a bit, make sure the shank is perfectly straight. A bit that does not spin true will shudder, producing a rough, imprecise cut. On carbide-tipped bits, also

Lubricating a router bit with a silicone-based lubricant before and after using it will help prevent the cutter from overheating.

inspect the brazing bond between the cutting edge and the shank. A bit with an uneven bond may fly apart under the stress of a cut. Other features are worth considering. For example, a bit boasting a nonstick coating like Teflon™ will take longer to become gummed up with pitch. You can also choose between piloted and non-piloted bits, cutters that feature anti-kick-back characteristics, and bits with spiral cutters.

Bits with different shank sizes perform different jobs. To shape an edge with a hand-held router, for example, a ¼-inch bit is usually appropriate. If you are using a bit with a ½-inch-diameter shank, mounting the router in a table will yield the best results. Large bits can be difficult to control in a hand-held router. Instead of using one large bit, however, you can make consecutive passes with two smaller bits.

EDGE-FORMING BITS

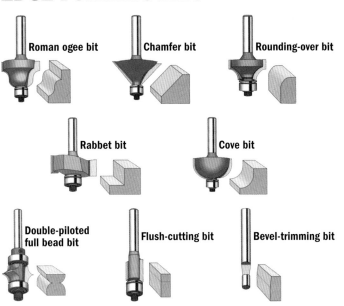

Roman ogee bit

Chamfer bit

Rounding-over bit

Rabbet bit

Cove bit

Double-piloted full bead bit

Flush-cutting bit

Bevel-trimming bit

ANATOMY OF A ROUTER BIT

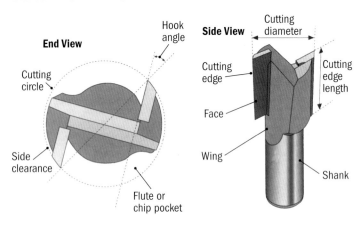

End View

Hook angle

Cutting circle

Side clearance

Flute or chip pocket

Side View

Cutting diameter

Cutting edge

Face

Wing

Cutting edge length

Shank

CHOOSING ROUTER BITS

There are several characteristics to look for when buying router bits. As it cuts through wood, a bit should only contact the workpiece with its cutting edges; the body should never touch the wood. A bit should also slice through wood with the edge of the cutter rather than the face. Two features make this possible. The first is the hook angle, which is the angle formed by the intersection between the cutting edge and the spinning axis of the bit. The second is bit shear. On bits with shear, the cutting edge is tilted vertically

A set of calipers measures the side clearance of a router bit, or the difference in diameter between the bit's cutting swath and the bit body. In a bit with adequate clearance, the bit body will not contact the workpiece as the cutting edges remove the waste.

with respect to the shank. Bits with shear and a hook angle of about 20° will produce a smooth cut with little tearout and are less likely to cause kickback.

Bits with anti-kickback, or chip-limiting, designs are becoming increasingly common. The cutters on these bits protrude from the bit body by only one-half as much as on a standard bit. By taking a shallower bite, the bits place less strain on the router motor. In addition, the bodies of these bits are virtually solid, with only a small gap between each cutting edge and the bit body. This reduces the risk of kickback.

Some straight bits are manufactured with a spiral design. Upcut spiral bits remove waste faster because they expel wood chips upward. Downcut spiral bits are slower, but they provide a cleaner cut.

GROOVING BITS

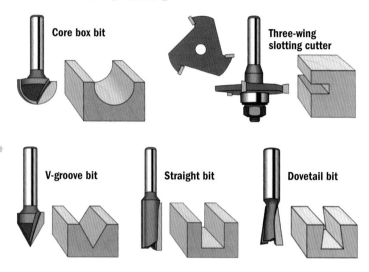

Core box bit

Three-wing slotting cutter

V-groove bit

Straight bit

Dovetail bit

*Shop*Tip

Chip-limitation bits
For wide cuts, chip-limitation bits are a safer alternative to the standard design. The cutters on these bits protrude from the bit body by only ¹⁄₁₆ inch—compared to the ⅛-inch typical of standard bits. By taking a shallower bite, the bits place less strain on the router motor. In addition, the bodies of chip-limitation bits are virtually solid, with only a ⅜-inch gap between the cutting edge and the bit body to allow for sharpening *(near right)*; this reduces the risk of kickback, often caused by the larger gap of standard bits *(far right)*.

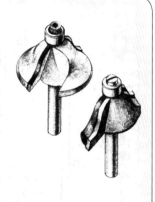

SHARPENING AND MAINTAINING BITS

Router bits require proper care. A cutter with excessive or uneven wear will perform poorly and can even be dangerous; it will tear at wood rather than cutting it cleanly, and can even pull the router out of your hands. A dirty or dull-edged bit can overheat, causing the bit to fracture.

A bit is being cleaned with commercial oven cleaner. For stubborn pitch and gum, the bit can be soaked in the cleaner in a shallow pan and scrubbed with a toothbrush.

Get in the habit of inspecting your bits periodically for damage, wear, and built-up dirt and pitch; use a magnifying glass, if necessary. A badly damaged bit should be discarded. As shown in the photo above, all you need to keep cutters clean is a toothbrush along with a cleaning agent, like turpentine, a mixture of hot water and ammonia, or commercial oven cleaner.

While most bit manufacturers suggest that their products be sharpened by professionals, the job can often be done in the shop. A bit with a properly sharpened edge can be maintained with an occasional honing. For best results with carbide cutting edges, use a diamond sharpening file. For high-speed steel bits, a benchstone is adequate.

There are times, however, when you should send out your bits to a professional sharpening service, particularly if the cutters have chipped edges or have lost their temper as a result of overheating.

ROUTER TABLE BITS

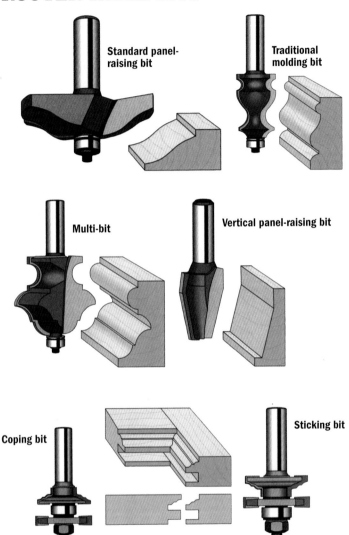

Standard panel-raising bit

Traditional molding bit

Multi-bit

Vertical panel-raising bit

Coping bit

Sticking bit

SHARPENING ROUTER BITS

Sharpening a non-piloted router bit

Use a benchstone to hone the inside faces of the cutting edges of a high-speed steel bit, like the one shown at right. Holding the inside face of one cutting edge flat against the abrasive surface, rub it back and forth. Repeat with the other edge. Hone both faces equally to maintain the balance of the bit.

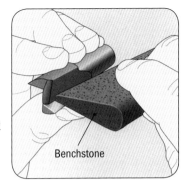

Benchstone

Sharpening a piloted bit

Remove the pilot bearing, then sharpen the bit as you would a non-piloted bit. For a carbide-tipped cutter like the one shown above, use a diamond sharpening file. Reinstall the bearing. If it does not rotate smoothly, spray a little bearing lubricant on it. If the bearing is worn out or damaged, replace it.

Diamond sharpening file

ACCESSORIES

The accessories illustrated at right are a sample of some commercial jigs and devices that make the router one of the most versatile tools in the workshop. Some of these products, like the foot switch, make the tool more convenient, especially for models with an on/off switch that cannot be reached while holding the handles. If you use such a device, however, be sure to disconnect it from the tool when you are changing a bit or performing any other maintenance.

Other accessories, such as the vacuum attachment, make the router a cleaner and safer tool. This attachment whisks away the sawdust and chips expelled by the router bit and directs them to your dust collection system.

Other accessories refine the router's cutting capabilities. The circle guide simplifies cutting circles, while template guides allow you to duplicate the profile of a template. A few of the devices on the market are designed to transform the router into another tool altogether. The plate joiner conversion kit gives you the ease and precision of biscuit joinery without the expense of buying a new tool, while the turning jig sets up a router for lathe work. But unlike an actual lathe, which spins the work for handcrafting, this accessory features a manual crank for rotating the workpiece while the spinning router bit shapes the wood.

A RANGE OF ROUTER ACCESSORIES

Vacuum attachment
Draws away sawdust and wood chips. One end attaches to tool base plate; the other end can be hooked up to a dust collection system. Compatible with only certain models.

Plate joiner conversion kit
Allows router to cut slots for plate or biscuit joints. Body of jig attaches to router base plate; kit includes compressed wood biscuits and three-wing slotting cutter.

Molding jig
For cutting moldings; router is fastened upright in a jig that is moved along surface of workpiece.

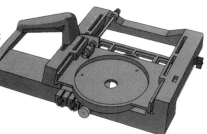

Universal base
For attaching accessories to router or mounting tool in router table; slots make base compatible with any router model.

A RANGE OF ROUTER ACCESSORIES *(continued)*

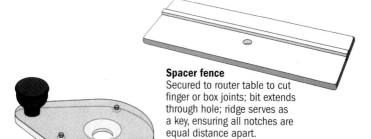

Spacer fence
Secured to router table to cut finger or box joints; bit extends through hole; ridge serves as a key, ensuring all notches are equal distance apart.

Offset router base
Helps keep router flat on workpiece while routing edges.

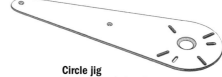

Circle jig
For routing circles. Router is attached to wide end while narrow end is screwed to workpiece; jig pivots around center of circle.

Router pad
A clamp substitute; rubberized mat holds stock in place on work surface.

A RANGE OF ROUTER
ACCESSORIES *(continued)*

Depth gauge
Used to set cutting depth of bit; features a series of steps in ¼-inch increments from ⅛ inch to 1 inch.

Template guides
Used for pattern routing; ride along template, allowing bit to replicate pattern. Sized for different-diameter bits, threaded part is secured to router base plate with ring.

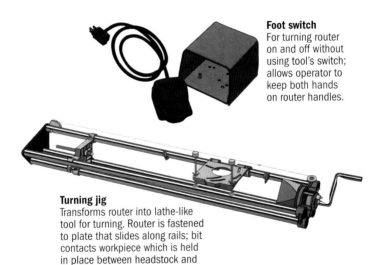

Foot switch
For turning router on and off without using tool's switch; allows operator to keep both hands on router handles.

Turning jig
Transforms router into lathe-like tool for turning. Router is fastened to plate that slides along rails; bit contacts workpiece which is held in place between headstock and tailstock and rotated by hand.

Router speed control
Allows variable control of router motor speed; useful when using larger bits that call for reduced rpm.

SETTING UP

A router cannot cut with precision unless it is properly set up and maintained. Changing a bit, for example, should be done with care—both to avoid damaging the cutting edges and to ensure that the bit is not sent flying when the tool is turned on. As shown in the photo at right, use the wrenches supplied with the tool to remove and install bits.

Installing a bit on most routers is a two-wrench operation. With the base plate removed, one wrench holds the shaft steady while the other loosens the collet. Position the wrenches so they can be squeezed together to provide extra leverage.

If a bit becomes stuck in the collet, gently strike the body of the bit with a wood scrap or tap the collet with a wrench. Do not try to extract the bit from the collet with pliers; this will damage the cutting edge. Before installing a new bit, clean any sawdust from the collet. Insert the replacement all the way into the collet, raise it about 1⁄16 inch, and tighten it in place.

The collet is one router component that may eventually need to be replaced. Periodically check your collet for bit slippage *(page 31)* and runout *(page 32)*, and change it if necessary.

SETTING THE CUTTING DEPTH

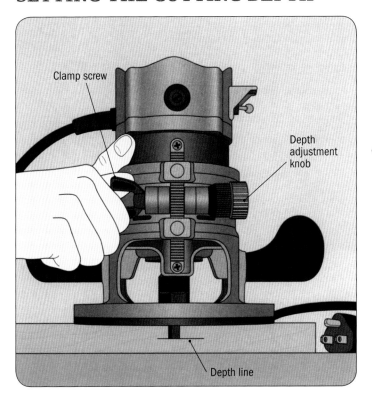

Clamp screw

Depth
adjustment
knob

Depth line

Adjusting a standard router

Set the router on the workpiece. For the model shown, loosen the clamp
screw and turn the depth adjustment knob to raise or lower the motor
and the bit. Align the tip of the bit with the depth line, then tighten the
clamp screw *(above)*. Alternatively, set the router upside down on a work
surface, loosen the clamp screw and rotate the depth adjustment knob
until the bit protrudes by the proper amount.

ADJUSTING A PLUNGE ROUTER

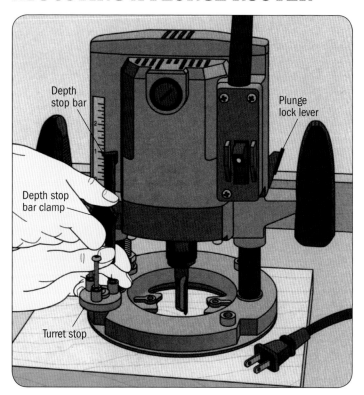

Depth stop bar

Plunge lock lever

Depth stop bar clamp

Turret stop

Set the router on the workpiece and rotate the turret stop on the router base to position the shortest stop screw directly under the depth stop bar. Loosen the depth stop bar clamp to release the bar and seat it on the stop screw. Then loosen the plunge lock lever and push the motor down until the bit contacts the workpiece. Tighten the lever and raise the stop bar until the gap between it and the stop screw equals the depth of cut (above). Tighten the depth stop bar clamp and loosen the plunge lock lever, allowing the motor and bit to spring back up. When

ADJUSTING A
PLUNGE ROUTER *(continued)*

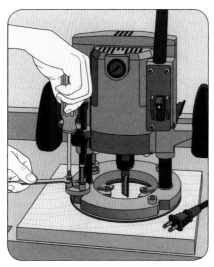

you plunge the bit into the stock, it will penetrate until the depth stop bar contacts the stop screw. For deep cuts, it is best to reach your final depth in stages. Set the height of the other two stop screws to make passes at intermediate depths by loosening the nut with a wrench and raising or lowering the screw with a screwdriver *(left)*.

---

*Shop*Tip

Checking a collet for slippage

To determine whether your router bits are slipping in the collet, install a bit and mark a line with a felt pen along the bit shank and collet. Then make a few cuts on a scrap board and examine the line. The marks on the bit and collet should be perfectly aligned. If they have shifted apart, the bit has slipped in the collet. Remove the bit and clean any pitch or sawdust out of the collet with a fine-bristled brass brush. Reinstall the bit, making sure it is well tightened, and retest. Replace the collet if the marks shift again.

CHECKING THE COLLET

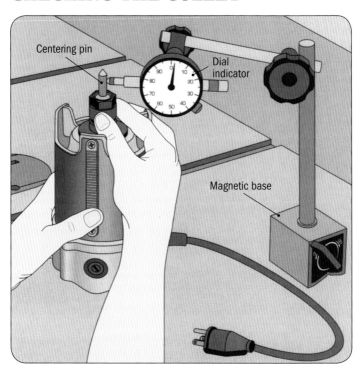

Centering pin

Dial indicator

Magnetic base

Using a dial indicator and magnetic base

Install a centering pin in the router as you would a bit and set the tool upside down on a metal surface, such as a table saw. Connect a dial indicator to a magnetic base and place the base next to the router. Turn on the magnet and position the router so the centering pin contacts the plunger of the dial indicator. Calibrate the dial indicator to zero following the manufacturer's instructions. Then turn the shaft of the router by hand to rotate the centering pin *(above)*. The dial indicator will register collet runout—the amount of wobble that the collet is giving the bit. If the runout exceeds 0.005 inch, replace the collet.

USING A FEELER GAUGE

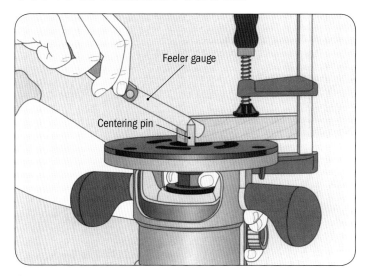

Feeler gauge

Centering pin

If you do not have a dial indicator, you can test for collet runout with a feeler gauge and a straight wood block. With the centering pin in the collet and the router upside down on a work surface, clamp the block lightly to the tool's sub-base so the piece cf wood touches the pin. Turn the router shaft by hand; any runout will cause the centering pin to move the block. Then use a feeler gauge to measure any gap between the pin and the block *(above)*. If the gap exceeds 0.005 inch, replace the collet.

STRAIGHT ROUTING

Using a piloted bit

Clamp the stock to a work surface with the edge you wish to shape extending off the table by a few inches. Gripping the router with both hands, rest its base plate on the workpiece at one end with the bit clear of the wood. Turn on the tool and ease the bit into the workpiece until the pilot contacts the edge, keeping the base plate flat on the stock and the pilot flush against the stock *(right)*. For deep cuts, make two or more passes to reach your final depth.

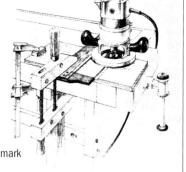

ShopTip

T-square router guide
To modify a drafting T-square into an edge guide for grooving cuts, clamp it to a scrap board with its crosspiece butted against the board edge. Then, with the router base plate riding along the arm of the square, rout a dado across the board and trim the crosspiece. To use the jig, clamp it to the workpiece with the cut edge of the crosspiece aligned with the cutting mark on the stock.

ROUTING WITH A NON-PILOTED BIT

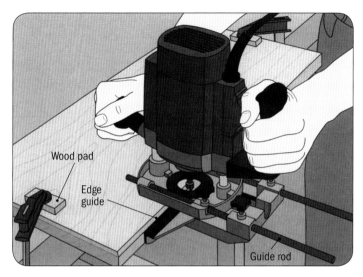

Install a commercial edge guide on the router, inserting the guide rods into the predrilled holes in the tool's base plate. Adjust the guide so the gap between the bit and the guide fence equals the width of cut. To make the cut, clamp the stock to your work surface. Then, keeping the guide fence flush against the edge to be shaped, start the cut at one end of the workpiece and draw the router along the edge *(above)*.

A SHOP-MADE SUB-BASE

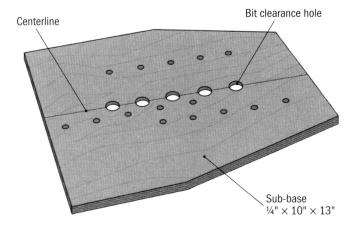

Centerline

Bit clearance hole

Sub-base
¼" × 10" × 13"

With its straight edge and large surface, the shop-made sub-base shown above ensures that your router will remain square to an edge guide clamped to the workpiece while you rout a series of equally spaced dadoes.

Using ¼-inch plywood, cut the sub-base about 10 inches wide and 13 inches long. Taper the sides so the end that rides along the edge guide is wider. Draw a line down the center of the sub-base. Starting near the wide end of the jig, mark a row of points for bit clearance holes; space the points 2 inches apart. Bore a hole at each mark; make sure

A SHOP-MADE SUB-BASE *(continued)*

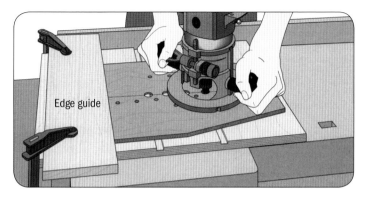

Edge guide

it is large enough for your largest straight bit. Unscrew the standard sub-base from your router and align its center with each of the bit clearance holes to mark the screw holes in the sub-base. Then bore these holes.

To use the jig, screw it to the router base plate so the bit passes through the first hole near the wide end. Align the bit with the cutting mark for the first dado on the workpiece, then butt an edge guide against the sub-base and clamp it in place. Rout the dado, keeping the sub-base flat on the stock and flush against the edge guide. Unscrew the sub-base from the router and reattach it so the bit protrudes from the appropriate hole and repeat to cut the next dado *(above)*.

A HINGED EDGE GUIDE

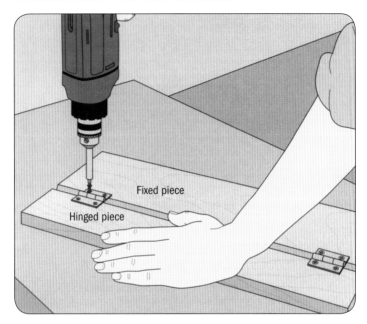

Fixed piece

Hinged piece

Making the guide

Although the distance from the center of the router bit to the base-plate edge is constant, remember that the distance from the bit's cutting edge to the base-plate edge will change with the diameter of each bit, and position your cutting lines accordingly. Or, you may want to make several hinged guides, each to be used with a specific bit. Built from ½ inch-thick stock, the guide can be aligned with a cutting mark on a workpiece and simply clamped in place. Cut the fixed part as you would a standard guide, but bevel the top of one edge to allow the hinged piece to pivot. Cut the hinged section so its width equals the distance between the bit's cutting edge and the edge of the router base plate. With their ends aligned and edges butted together, fasten the two pieces of the guide using butt hinges *(above)*.

USING THE GUIDE

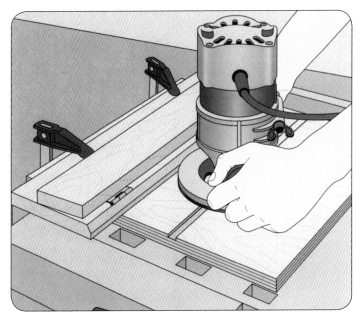

To make a dado cut, set the edge guide on your workpiece and line up the edge of the hinged section with the cutting mark. Clamp the fixed section in place. Then flip up the hinged section and rout the channel, keeping the router base plate flush against the fixed piece *(above)*.

ROUTER TABLES

Mounted upside down in a specially designed table, a router cuts a dado. Attaching a backup board to the miter gauge helps keep the work square to the bit and reduces tearout.

Although your router is a remarkably versatile tool, its usefulness can be extended even further by mounting it in a table. Stationary routing frees your hands to feed stock into the bit, allowing you to exert greater control over the cutting operation. Since a typical router bit spins at 20,000 rpm or faster, this extra margin of safety is welcome. In addition, some bits should only be used on a table-mounted router. These bits have large cutting heads that exert high forces against the workpiece, requiring an extra measure of control.

A router table is an excellent substitute for a light-duty shaper, and commercial models are available in many sizes and configurations.

ROUTER TABLES *(continued)*

Most tables have a guard to cover the bit and an adjustable fence for guiding stock into the cut. If you would like a customized table, you can easily build your own following the designs beginning on page 44.

Cutting depth on a router table depends on how far the bit protrudes above the work surface, while the width of cut is determined by how much of the bit extends beyond the fence. On commercial tables, the fence is usually split. The two halves are normally left in alignment for partial cuts. When you are routing the full edge of a workpiece, however, start with the fences aligned, but then stop the cut a few inches into it. Advance the outfeed fence so it touches the cut portion, then complete the operation.

---

*Shop*Tip

A router table on the table saw

To make the most of the space in a small shop, build a router table into your table saw's extension table. Rout a ¼-inch-deep recess into the top of the extension table and cut a piece of ¼-inch-thick acrylic plastic to fit into the depression. Drill a hole in the center of the plastic larger than your biggest router bit. With a saber saw, cut a hole in the recess to accommodate your router's base plate. Then remove the base plate from the tool and screw it to the plastic piece. Next screw the plastic into the recess; countersink all the fasteners. Reattach the router to the base plate. A fence for the router table can be cut from plywood and attached to the saw fence when necessary.

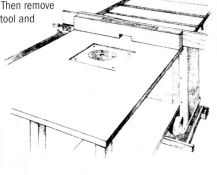

SETTING UP A COMMERCIAL ROUTER TABLE

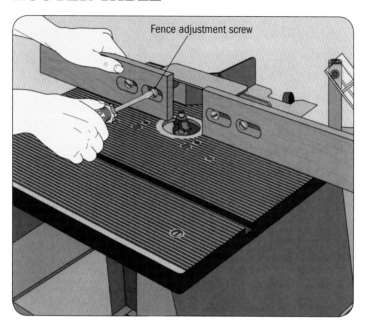

Fence adjustment screw

Adjusting the fence

Mount the router in the table. On the model shown, you need to remove the base plate from the tool and fasten the plate underneath the table. The bit is then installed in the router and the tool is reattached to the base plate. To set up the fence for a cut, loosen the four adjustment screws *(above)* and move the two halves of the fence as close as possible to the bit without touching the cutting edges. Tighten the screws, then set the width of cut. Move the fence back from the bit for a wide pass; for a shallower cut, shift the fence closer to the bit. If you are using a piloted bit and want to make a cut equal to the full diameter of the bit, use a straightedge to line up the fence with the outside edge of the pilot bearing, then tighten the adjustment screws.

MAKING A CUT

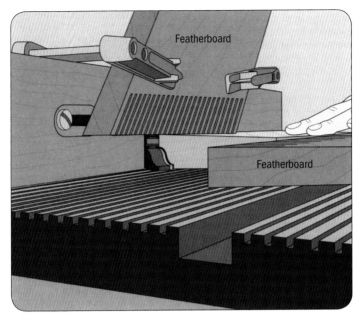

Featherboard

Featherboard

To support a workpiece properly and avoid kickback as you feed stock into the bit, clamp one featherboard to the fence above the cutter, and a second featherboard to the table in line with the bit. Always feed stock into the cutter against the direction of bit rotation. With the workpiece clear of the bit, turn on the router and slowly feed the stock into the cutting edge while holding it flush against the fence *(above)*. To keep your fingers safely away from the bit, finish the pass with a push stick. Position the guard over the bit whenever possible.

SHOP-MADE ROUTER TABLES

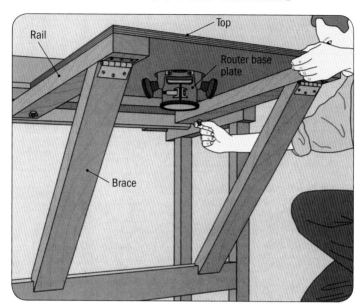

Rail
Top
Router base plate
Brace

An extension router table

Attached to a workbench, the compact router table shown above can be easily removed when it is not needed. Size the parts according to your needs. Start by cutting the top from ¾-inch plywood, and the rails and braces from 2-by-4 stock. Saw the rails a few inches longer than the width of the top so they can be fastened to the underside of the workbench using wing nuts and hanger bolts *(above)*. The hinged braces should be long enough to reach from the underside of the rails to a leg stretcher on the bench. Cut a bevel at the top end of the braces and a right-angled notch at the bottom end. The router is attached to the top with a square sub-base of ¼-inch clear acrylic. Several steps are necessary to fit the sub-base to the top and then to the router. First, clamp the sub-base to the center of the top and outline its edges with a pencil. Mark the center of the sub-base and drill a pilot hole through

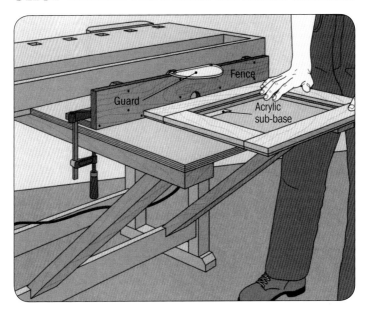

the acrylic and the top. Remove the sub-base and rout out a ¼-inch-deep recess within the outline. Then, using the pilot hole as a center, cut a round hole through the top to accommodate your router's base plate. To prepare the sub-base, drill a hole through its center that is slightly larger than your largest router bit, then fasten the sub-base to the router using machine screws. Set the sub-base in the table recess and attach it with wood screws; countersink all the fasteners. For a fence, cut two pieces of ¾-inch plywood and screw them together in an L shape; add triangular supports as shown on page 44. Saw a notch out of the fence's bottom edge large enough for your largest bit. Attach a clear semicircular plastic guard with a hinge to allow it to be flipped out of the way. To use the router table, clamp the fence in position and feed the workpiece into the bit, holding it flush against the fence *(above)*.

A SHOP-MADE ROUTER TABLE/CABINET

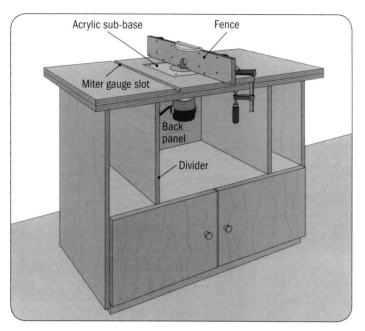

Acrylic sub-base

Fence

Miter gauge slot

Back panel

Divider

Built entirely from ¾-inch plywood, the table shown below allows you to use your router as a stationary molding, shaping, and grooving tool. It features a spacious tabletop with a slot for a miter gauge, an adjustable fence, a storage shelf, and cupboards. Start with the basic structure of the table, sizing the bottom, sides, back, shelf, and doors to suit your needs. Fix these parts together, using the joinery method of your choice. The table shown is assembled with biscuit joints. Bore a hole through the back panel to accommodate the router's power cord. For the top, cut two pieces of plywood and use glue and screws to fasten them together; the pieces should be large enough to overhang the sides by 2 or 3 inches. Cut the dividers to fit between the top and the shelf, then fix them in place.

A SHOP-MADE ROUTER TABLE/CABINET *(continued)*

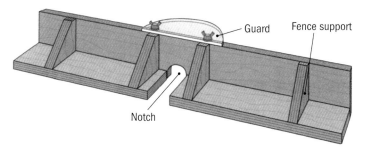

Use an acrylic sub-base to attach the router to the tabletop as you would for a removable table *(page 44)*. Also, use the same type of L-shaped fence with a guard, a notch for the bit, and four triangular supports screwed to the back for extra stability; the guard on this fence is fixed in place with bolts and wing nuts, rather than a hinge *(above)*. Use the fence to help you rout the miter gauge slot across the top: Clamp the fence square to the front edge of the top and guide the router along it as you plow the slot.

A SHOP-MADE ROUTER TABLE/CABINET *(continued)*

Featherboard

Push stick

The router table can be used the same way as a commercial model *(page 42)*. For edge-forming operations, set the width of cut by clamping the fence the appropriate distance from the bit *(above)*.

A SHOP-MADE ROUTER
TABLE/CABINET *(continued)*

Be sure to use featherboards to support your workpiece and a push stick to finish the pass. To make a cut on the inside edges of a cabinet or door frame, remove the fence. Then, holding the frame firmly, butt its inside edge against the bit near one corner and rotate it clockwise to make the cut *(above)*. Keep the frame flat on the table as you feed it into the bit.

THE ROUTER AS SURFACER

A Plug-Trimming Jig

Wood plug

Hardboard
sub-base

Runner

Cutting plugs flush

Equipped with the jig shown above, a router with a straight or mortising
bit can make quick work of trimming protruding wood plugs or dowels
flush with the surface of a workpiece. To fashion the jig, unscrew the
sub-base from your router and use it as a template to cut a slightly larger
replacement from ¼-inch hardboard. Bore holes through the new sub-base
for the bit and mounting screws. Cut two runners from ¾-inch hardwood
and fasten them to the sub-base using glue and nails, then screw the jig
to the router base plate. To use the jig, hold it over the workpiece and lower
the bit until the tip contacts the surface. Then switch the router on and slide
the runners over the workpiece to trim the plugs flush with the surface.

ShopTip

Surfacing small workpieces

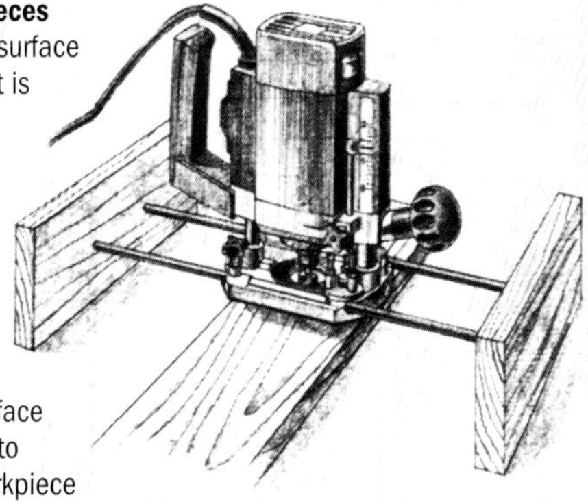

A router can be used to surface small workpieces when it is equipped with the jig shown here. The device consists of hardwood blocks fixed to metal rods that fit snugly in the edge-guide mounting holes of the router base plate. Set your stock on a work surface and nail or screw cleats to the table against the workpiece to keep it in place. Install a ¾-inch-diameter straight bit in the router and, holding the tool over the stock, lower the bit until it contacts the lowest point on the surface. Starting at one end of the workpiece, turn on the router and move it over the surface, sliding the blocks along the table. Make as many overlapping passes as necessary until you reach the other end.

A SURFACING JIG

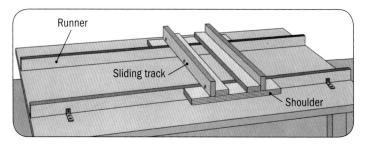

Used with the jig shown above, your router becomes a surfacing tool for
large pieces of rough stock. Built from ¾-inch plywood, the jig consists
of a track for the router that slides along two runners fixed to a work
table. Cut the runners 3 inches wide and long enough to span the table.
Fasten the runners to the table using angle brackets; make the space
between the runners sufficient for the widest stock you will surface.
The sliding track consists of six pieces. The four pieces that support
the router should be 3 inches wide and long enough to overhang the
runners by a few inches on each side. Screw these pieces together in
an L shape. Cut the shoulders about 4 inches wide and 12 inches long
and screw them to the router supports so the shoulders slide against
the outside of the runners; make the sliding track ¾ inch wider than the
router base plate.

A SURFACING JIG *(continued)*

To use the jig, set the workpiece to be surfaced on the table between the runners and secure it in place with double-sided tape or cleats nailed to the table. Install a ¾-inch-diameter straight bit in the router and seat the tool in the sliding track. Lower the bit until it contacts the lowest point on the surface. Starting at one end of the workpiece, hold the router firmly and turn it on. Slide the tool along one of the vertical supports and back along the other one to make a 1½-inch-wide pass, then advance the sliding track along the runners *(above)*. Make as many passes as necessary at successive depths along the length of the workpiece until it is evenly surfaced.

CHAPTER 2:

The shaped edge of a workpiece often provides the final, finishing touch: a crown molding adorning an armoire top, a crisp bevel on a raised panel, an ogee cut around the edge of a tabletop. These decorative flourishes were once created painstakingly by hand, using planes and spokeshaves; today they are invariably made with an array of electric woodworking tools, chief among them the portable router. This chapter outlines both basic and advanced edge-forming techniques, from pattern routing to making molding.

Stationary power tools such as the jointer and table saw can cut rabbets, and the table saw can also shape decorative edges, but the router is the most versatile, efficient tool for the job. Utilizing a wide range of interchangeable cutters, it can also make cuts that are impossible to perform with any other power tool; imagine forming a decorative bead around the inside of a circular picture frame without a router.

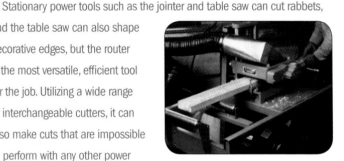

Combining the solidity of a planer with the versatility of a shaper, the molding planer is capable of assembly-line type production of many types of molding, from straight to curved.

Edge-forming bits often have ball-bearing pilots that ride along the stock to maintain uniform cutter depth. Here, a double-fluted beading bit carves a decorative profile around the circumference of a tabletop.

Commercial accessories and shop-made jigs expand the router's ability to shape edges still further. A simple corner-rounding jig *(page 62)* can round tabletops or shelves to your specifications. A flush-trimming guide *(page 66)* helps you trim solid wood edge banding applied to core stock. A veneer trimmer *(page 68)* proves handy for preparing veneer for book-matching.

Mounting the router in a table or pin routing attachment enables you to create more complex edge profiles and elaborate curves. It also provides the stability needed for raising panels *(page 74)*, an edge-forming technique that can also be accomplished on die table saw, radial arm saw, and drill press.

The pin router is perhaps the ultimate shop tool for complex edge-forming tasks *(page 66)*. Essentially an inverted router table, the tool features a pin projecting from the tabletop directly under the bit along which the stock is guided, making the tool ideal for template work. A shop-made pin routing attachment is easily built and adaptable to most commercial router tables *(page 63)*. Remember, too, that not all edge forming must be done with a router. By installing a molding head on the table saw or radial arm saw you can rout detailed moldings.

BASIC EDGE SHAPING

Making multiple copies of the same contoured shape with the router requires the use of a straightedge, a jig, or a template to guide the tool along the edge of a workpiece.

With a template, your router can make quick work of repeating a curved cut in a series of workpieces. The exact procedure you follow depends on the type of bit you are using. With a piloted bit, the cutting edge is below the pilot and the template

A support board secured alongside a workpiece during an edge-forming operation keeps the router steady. For contour cuts, use the waste piece that remains after sawing the curve.

is clamped atop the workpiece. The pilot will follow the curved edge of the template while the cutters reproduce the same curve on the workpiece.

When you use a non-piloted bit, attach a template guide to the router base plate. The guide is a metal collar that surrounds the bit shank and protrudes slightly from the bottom of the router's sub-base. With the template secured atop the stock, the guide rides along the edge of the pattern, enabling the bit to shape the workpiece.

Whichever type of bit you use, make the template from durable wood, such as plywood or particleboard. Cut the pattern using a band saw or a saber saw, then carefully sand the edges that will be guiding the router.

For a non-piloted bit, make the template slightly thicker than the height of the template guide. With a piloted bit, the template should be thick enough to provide an adequate bearing surface for the pilot.

PATTERN ROUTING WITH A PILOTED BIT

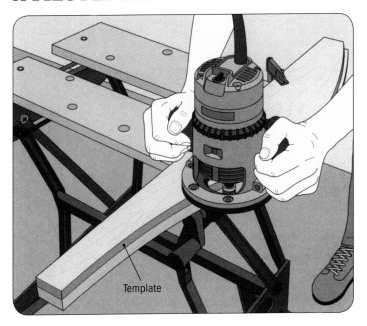

Template

Making the cut

Make a template that is precisely the same size as the finished pieces you wish to cut. Use the template to outline the pattern on your workpiece, then cut out most of the waste with a band saw or saber saw, leaving about ⅟₁₆ inch of stock beyond the cutting line. Use double-sided tape to fasten the workpiece to the template, ensuring that the straight edges of the boards are aligned. Clamp the two pieces to a work surface. Holding the router with both hands, rest its base plate on the template at one end with the bit clear of the wood and turn on the tool. Ease the bit into the stock until the pilot contacts the edge, then pull the router toward the other end of the cut, keeping the base plate flat on the template and the pilot flush against its edge *(above)*.

USING A TEMPLATE GUIDE

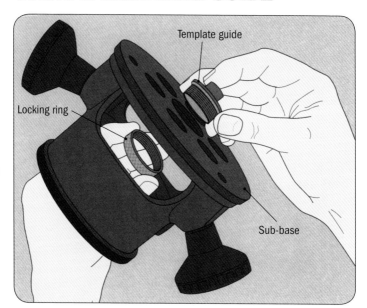

Template guide

Locking ring

Sub-base

Installing a template guide

Loosen the clamp screw on the router base plate and remove the plate.
Insert the threaded part of the template guide through the hole in the
middle of the sub-base *(above)*, then screw on the locking ring to hold
the two together. The diameter of the template guide should be as
close to that of the bit as possible without touching the cutting edges.
Reassemble the router.

MAKING THE CUT

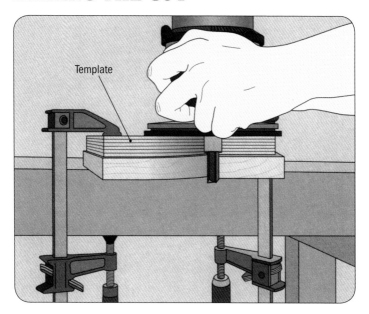

Template

Prepare a template that is slightly smaller than the finished piece
to compensate for the difference between the bit diameter and the
diameter of the template guide. Fasten the template atop the workpiece
with double-sided tape, then clamp the two pieces to a work surface.
Cut the pattern as you would with a piloted bit, feeding the cutter into
the stock until the template guide contacts the template. Complete
the cut, making sure that the guide is pressed against the edge of the
pattern throughout the operation *(above)*.

ROUNDING CORNERS

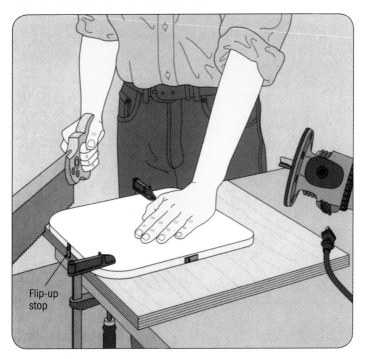

Flip-up
stop

Sawing the excess waste

You can use a commercial corner-rounding jig to curve the corners of
a workpiece. Set your stock on a work surface and place the jig atop
the corner to be rounded. Set the flip-up stops on the jig in the vertical
position to align the edges of the jig with those of the workpiece. Clamp
the two pieces to the work surface. To make the router cut easier, saw
away the bulk of the waste *(above)*.

ROUNDING THE CORNER

Using a top-piloted flush-cutting bit, start clear of the corner, making the cut as you would when pattern routing with a piloted bit *(page 34)*. Keep the bit pilot pressed against the edge of the jig throughout the operation *(above)*.

UNDERSIDE VIEW

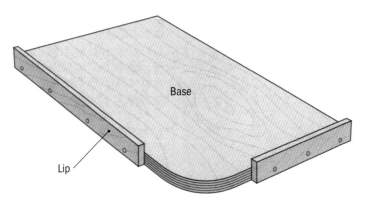

Base

Lip

A Corner-Rounding Jig

Easy and inexpensive to build, the corner-rounding jig at left works as well as the commercial version shown on the previous page. The jig consists of a plywood base and two lips that keep the edges of the jig and the workpiece aligned.

Cut the base from a piece of ¾-inch plywood. For most jobs, a base about 10 inches wide and 16 inches long will be adequate. Draw the curve you wish to rout on the base near one corner, then make the cut with a band saw or a saber saw; sand the edge smooth. You can also cut the corner using a router attached to a circle-cutting guide *(page 97)*.

Cut the lips from stock ½ inch thick and 1½ inches wide, then nail or screw the pieces to the base, leaving about 3 to 4 inches between each lip and the rounded corner. The top edge of the lips should be flush with the top surface of the base.

To use the jig, set your stock on a work surface with the corner to be rounded extending off the table by several inches. Place the jig on top of the workpiece so the lips are butted against the edges of the stock. Use clamps to secure the two pieces to the work surface. Make the cut as you would with a commercial jig, pressing the bit's pilot against the edge of the jig throughout *(above)*.

CUTTING AND TRIMMING PLASTIC LAMINATES

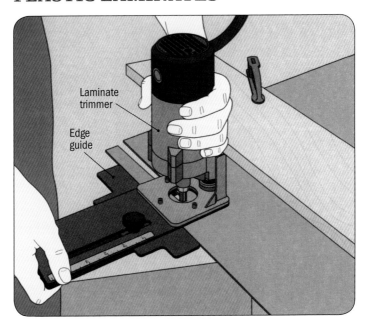

Laminate trimmer

Edge guide

Cutting strips of edging

Use a laminate trimmer with a commercial edge guide to cut strips of edging from a sheet of laminate. The guide ensures that the width of each strip is uniform. Attach the guide to the trimmer (on the model shown, the trimmer's sub-base is removed and the edge guide is fastened to the tool's base plate); then adjust the width of cut following the manufacturer's instructions. Install a straight bit in the trimmer and clamp the sheet to a work surface, using a board to keep the sheet flat. With the bit clear of the sheet, start the cut at one end. Holding the trimmer with one hand, feed the tool toward the opposite end; use your other hand to press the guide flush against the edge of the sheet *(above)*.

INSTALLING AND TRIMMING THE LAMINATE

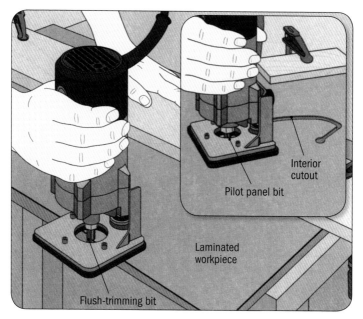

Interior cutout

Pilot panel bit

Laminated workpiece

Flush-trimming bit

Glue the banding onto the edges of the workpiece and clamp the panel edge-up. Remove the edge guide from the trimmer and install the sub-base and a flush-cutting bit. Use the tool to trim any banding that projects beyond the edges of the workpiece. Repeat to glue and trim edging on the ends of the panel. Glue the top laminate in place next. To trim it flush with the edges, hold the trimmer firmly with one hand and guide the tool along the workpiece *(above)*. To make an interior cut to match a cutout in the panel, clamp the panel to the work surface. Install a pilot panel bit in the trimmer and plunge the bit's sharpened tip into the sheet to pierce it, then feed the trimmer until the pilot contacts the edge of the cutout. Making sure that the pilot remains flush against the edge of the cutout *(inset)*, complete the cut.

A FLUSH-TRIMMING JIG

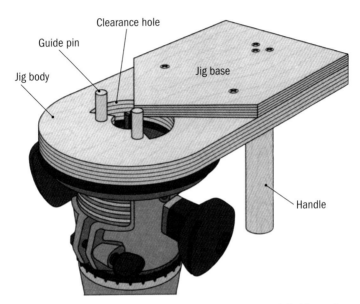

The jig shown at right allows you to use a non-piloted straight bit to trim solid edge banding flush with the top and bottom surfaces of a panel. Designed to be screwed to the tool's sub-base, the jig features two guide pins that ride along the outside face of the banding while the end of the bit trims the banding.

To make the jig, cut the base from ½-inch plywood and the body from ¾-inch plywood. Make the width of both pieces equal to the diameter of your router base plate; cut the body about 12 inches long and the base 8 inches long. Use the tool's sub-base as a template to cut the curve at one end of the jig body. Also, cut a 3-inch-diameter hole through the body to clear the bit, but leave a section within the circle to house the guide pins. Cut one end of the jig base to a point, then screw the base to the jig body; countersink the fasteners. Bore two

A FLUSH-TRIMMING JIG *(continued)*

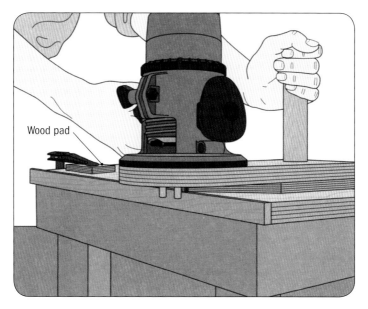

Wood pad

⅝-inch-diameter holes through the wedge in the body and glue two short lengths of dowels in the holes; position the holes so the bit will line up directly over the edge of the banding with the guide pins flush against the stock. To complete the jig, cut a length of dowel for a handle and screw it to the body.

To use the jig, attach the router's sub-base to the body with screws. Install a straight bit in the tool and adjust the cutting depth so the tip of the bit is level with the bottom of the jig base. Clamp your stock to a work surface, protecting it with a wood pad. With the bit clear of the workpiece, turn on the router and set the jig base on the top of the stock. Butting the guide pins against the outside surface of the banding, guide the router along the top edge, trimming the banding *(above)*. Apply downward pressure on the handle throughout the operation to keep the router from tipping.

A VENEER-TRIMMING GUIDE

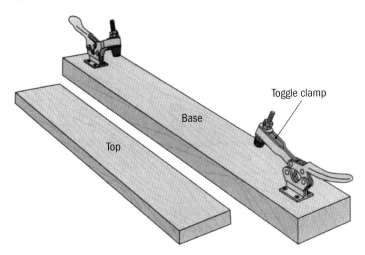

Toggle clamp

Base

Top

Trim sheets of veneer to width quickly and accurately on a router table with the jig shown at right. The veneer is sandwiched between the base and top of the jig; the base rides along the pilot of a flush-cutting bit, which cuts the veneer flush with the edge of the jig *(above)*.

Cut the base from 1½-inch-thick stock and the top from ¾-inch-thick stock. Make the pieces about 6 inches wide; the base should be a few inches longer than your router table, and the top long enough to cover the veneer. Choose a board with a slight bow for the top, if possible; with the bow facing down, applying clamping pressure near the ends of

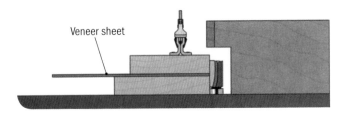

Veneer sheet

A VENEER-TRIMMING GUIDE (continued)

Guard

the board will flatten it, producing uniform pressure against the base. Screw toggle clamps to the base so the top will fit between them.

To prepare your router table for the operation, install the bit on the router and mount the tool in the table. Cut a guard from a piece of stock, sawing a notch from one edge to form a lip that will cover the cutter. Clamp the guard to the table.

To use the jig, place the veneer to be trimmed between the base and the top so the grain of the veneer is parallel to that of the boards. The edges of the sheets should protrude from the jig by about ⅛ inch. Press the toggle clamps down on the top to secure the veneer sheets to the jig. Turn on the router and slide the jig across the table to cut the veneer (above), keeping the jig pressed against the pilot throughout the operation.

UNDERCUTTING CURVED EDGES

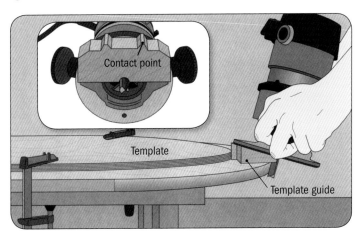

Contact point

Template

Template guide

Using a shop-made template guide

This technique enables you to undercut the perimeter of a circular workpiece using a straight bit. To make the guide, cut a bevel across the face of a wood block. Make the width of the guide equal to the distance between the bit and the edge of the router sub-base. Saw two triangular contact points 1 inch apart in the guide's outside edge *(inset)*; also cut a notch out of the inside edge to accommodate the bit. Install a straight bit in the router and screw the jig to the router's base. Clamp a template atop the workpiece so that the distance between the template and the workpiece's edge is the same as that between the bit and the contact points of the guide. Make the cut *(above)*, keeping the contact points flush against the template throughout the operation. Reposition the template as necessary to finish the cut.

ShopTip

A flush-trimming device

You do not have to buy a laminate trimmer to trim laminate edge banding applied to core stock. The simple commercial device shown here does the job with a couple of small blades contained in a spring-mounted housing. Squeeze the two halves of the tool together until they fit snugly against the workpiece and then draw the device from one end of the board to the other. The blades will trim away any excess banding, leaving you with perfectly flush edges.

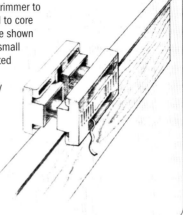

ShopTip

Jointing wide boards

If you have boards that are too cumbersome to move across the jointer, you can undertake the task with a router and a perfectly square edge guide. Install a ½-inch top-piloted flush-trimming bit in a router with a ½-inch collet. Position the edge guide atop the board to be jointed and clamp the pieces to a work-bench with the edge of the board protruding from the guide's edge by about ¹/₁₆ inch. Feed the router from one end of the board to the other; the pilot will ride along the guide as the cutter trims the board flush.

JOINTING ON A ROUTER TABLE

Jointing an edge

Install a straight bit in the router with a cutting edge longer than the thickness of your workpiece, and mount the tool in a router table. To remove 1⁄16 inch of wood from your stock—a typical amount when jointing—adjust the position of the fence for a cut of that amount. Make a test cut in a scrap board, then unplug the router and hold the board in place against the fence. Loosen the outfeed fence thumbscrews and advance the outfeed half until it butts against the cut part of the board *(top)*. Tighten the thumbscrews. Butt the workpiece against the fence a few inches back from the bit and then slowly feed the board into the cutter, keeping your hand clear of the bit and pressing the workpiece firmly against the fence *(bottom)*.

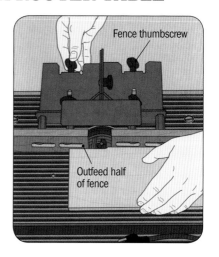

Fence thumbscrew

Outfeed half of fence

Apply side pressure just to the outfeed side of the bit. For narrow stock, finish the cut with a push stick.

JOINTING WITH A ROUTER TABLE

Setting up the table

Install a straight bit in the router, with a cutting edge longer than the thickness of your workpiece. To remove $\frac{1}{16}$ inch of wood from your stock—a typical amount when jointing—adjust the position of the fence for a cut of that amount. Make a test cut a few inches into a scrap board, then hold the board in place

Fence thumb-screw

Outfeed half of fence

against the fence. For a router with an adjustable split fence, loosen the fence thumbscrews *(right)* and advance the outfeed half until it butts against the cut part of the stock. Tighten the thumbscrews. If your router table has a one-piece fence, fasten a strip of veneer on the outfeed side the same width as the amount of stock removed in the test cut.

Jointing an edge

Butt the workpiece against the router table fence a few inches from the bit. Slowly feed the stock into the cutter *(right)*, while keeping it pressed snugly against the fence. Apply side pressure just to the outfeed side of the bit.

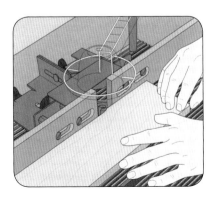

RAISING PANELS

Frame-and-panel construction is a clever way of getting around the fact that wood shrinks and swells with changes in humidity. The principle is simple: The panel "floats" within the frame, sitting in grooves cut around its inside edges. Cutting a bevel around the edge of the panel allows the piece to fit into the grooves in the frame and gives a decorative "raised" effect to the main part of the panel.

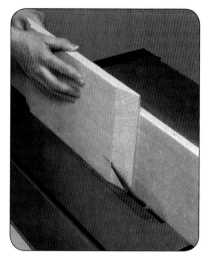

Panels can be raised on a number of stationary woodworking tools; a table saw with a tilting arbor works well. An auxiliary wood fence makes the job safer and more accurate.

Traditionally, panels were raised with special planes that featured angled and profiled cutters and soles. That job could require hours of arduous work, especially if the wood was dense, such as oak, maple, or cherry. Today you can raise panels on the table saw, radial arm saw, drill press, and shaper.

Panel raising is often done on the router table with one of several specially designed router bits *(page 22)*. These cutters can handle stock up to ¾ inch thick, but the bits' large diameter—typically 3½ inches—can make the workpiece difficult to control. If you plan to do a lot of panel raising, consider building a jig for the task *(page 80)*.

Since raising panels involves removal of a good deal of stock, it is best not to attempt to make the cut in one pass. Instead, make a series of partial passes, increasing the depth of cut gradually each time, until the panel is ¼ inch thick at the edges or fits snugly in the grooves cut in the frame.

POPULAR RAISED PANEL DESIGNS

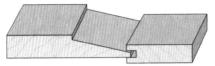

Beveled panel raised from frame

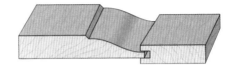

Ogee beveled panel

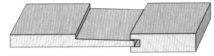

Beveled panel flush with frame

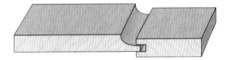

Cove

Recessed panel with rabbets

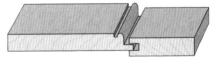

Bead

RAISING PANELS ON THE ROUTER TABLE

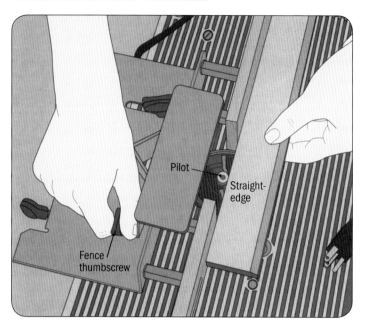

Using a piloted panel-raising bit

Install a piloted panel-raising bit in your router and mount the tool in a router table. With the router turned off, loosen the four fence adjustment screws and move the two halves of the fence as close as possible to the bit without touching the cutting edges. Tighten the screws. To ensure that the width of cut is uniform, position the fence in line with the edge of the bit pilot: Loosen the thumbscrews behind the fence, then hold a straightedge against the fence and move both halves together until the straightedge contacts the pilot. The pilot should turn as the edge touches it *(above)*; adjust the fence's position, if necessary, then tighten the thumbscrews. Set the

RAISING PANELS ON
THE ROUTER TABLE *(continued)*

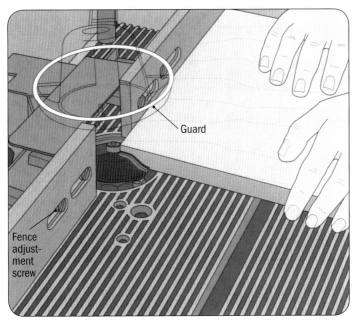

Guard

Fence adjustment screw

router for a ⅛-inch depth of cut, lower the guard over the bit and turn on the router. For added stability, you can clamp a featherboard to each half of the fence to press the panel against the table. (In the illustrations on this page, the featherboards have been removed for clarity.) To minimize tearout, cut into the end grain of the panel first, beveling the ends before the sides. With the outside face of the panel down on the table, feed the stock into the bit, pushing it forward with your right hand and keeping it flush against the fence with your left *(above)*. Test-fit the panel in the frame grooves and make subsequent passes, increasing the cutting depth by a maximum of ⅛ inch each time.

USING A NON-PILOTED VERTICAL PANEL-RAISING BIT

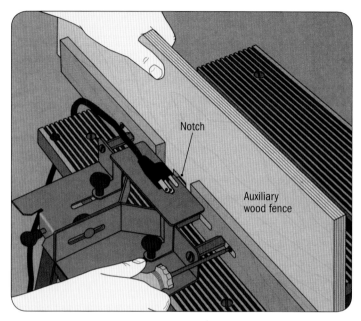

Notch

Auxiliary
wood fence

In this operation, the panel will be fed across the bit in an upright
position, so you must attach a high auxiliary wood fence *(above)*.
Make the fence about 8 inches high and cut a notch in the middle to
accommodate the bit. For this cut, the cutting depth depends on the
amount by which the bit protrudes from the fence. To begin, set the fence

USING A NON-PILOTED VERTICAL PANEL-RAISING BIT *(continued)*

Featherboard

Shim

for a ⅛-inch depth of cut. To secure the panel, clamp a featherboard to the table; rest the featherboard on a shim to keep the panel from tilting as you run it past the bit. Feed the panel with your right hand while pressing it flat against the fence with your left *(above)*. Cut the top and bottom of the panel first, then the sides. Back the fence from the bit no more than ⅛ inch at a time for further, deeper passes until the panel fits into the groove.

A PANEL-RAISING JIG

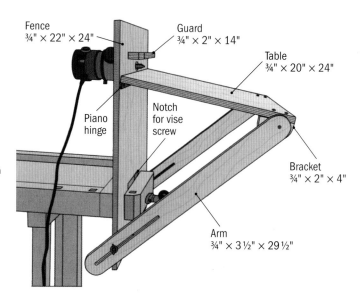

Fence
¾" × 22" × 24"

Guard
¾" × 2" × 14"

Table
¾" × 20" × 24"

Piano
hinge

Notch
for vise
screw

Bracket
¾" × 2" × 4"

Arm
¾" × 3½" × 29½"

The shop-made jig above allows you to raise panels without mounting
your router in a table. Featuring a tilting table and a fence to which
the router is attached, the jig is secured to a workbench tail vise. This
provides a safe, accurate way to mill a wide range of profiles.

Cut all the pieces of the jig from ¾-inch plywood; the dimensions
suggested in the illustration will work well with the typical workbench.
Start assembling the jig by screwing the brackets to the underside
of the table at one end. Cut adjustment slots through the arms, then
bolt the top ends of the arms to the brackets and the bottom ends
to the fence using hanger bolts, washers, and wing nuts. Attach the
table to the fence with a piano hinge positioned about 6 inches
below the top of the fence. To prepare the fence for your router, bore

A PANEL-RAISING JIG (continued)

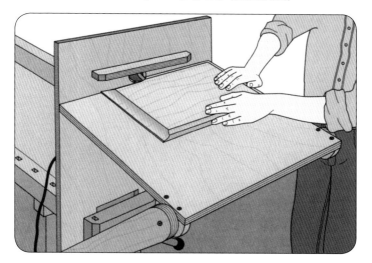

a hole just above the table level that will accommodate your largest vertical panel-raising bit. Screw the guard to the fence above the hole. Finally, cut a notch into the bottom end of the fence to clear the vise screw.

To use the jig, secure it in the vise so the table is at a comfortable working height. Install a ½-inch vertical panel-raising bit in the router, then screw the base plate to the fence so the bit protrudes from the hole. Adjusting the bit for a shallow cut, turn on the router and make a test cut in a scrap piece. To adjust the bevel angle, turn off the tool, loosen the wing nuts securing the arms to the fence and tilt the table up or down. As on the router table, cut the bevels on the ends of the panel before those on the sides. Feed the panel across the table face-up *(above)*, keeping your fingers clear of the bit. Test-fit the panel and increase the cutting depth by ⅛ inch for a second pass.

THE ROUTER AS SHAPER

Fitted with a chamfering bit and suspended upside down in a specially designed table, a router becomes a stationary tool—in this case, cutting a decorative V-groove for a tongue-and-groove joint.

With its bit whirring at 20,000 rpm or faster, the router can be somewhat intimidating. Among the many benefits of installing your router in a table is the extra margin of safety such an arrangement provides. Solidly mounted to a table with its bit barely projecting above the work surface, the router seems much more manageable.

The router table adds a range of versatility that no other single accessory can provide. Among other things, it frees your hands to feed stock into the tool, allowing you to exert greater control on the

THE ROUTER AS SHAPER *(continued)*

cutting operation. In addition, there are bits that can only be used on a table-mounted router. While some of the cutters shown in the illustration below—the beading bit, for instance—can also be used in hand-held work, router table bits are generally significantly larger, giving you much greater flexibility when preparing stock for joinery or cutting decorative shapes.

Commercial router tables are available in many sizes and configurations. All models have a guard to cover the bit; many feature an adjustable fence and a groove for a miter gauge. Cutting depth on a router table depends on how far the bit protrudes; the width of cut will depend on how much of the bit extends beyond the fence. On commercial tables, the fence is commonly split. The two halves are normally left in alignment for shallow cuts; the outfeed fence can be set behind the infeed fence for more aggressive removal of stock. For a customized router table, you can also build your own *(page 44)*.

Router Table Bits

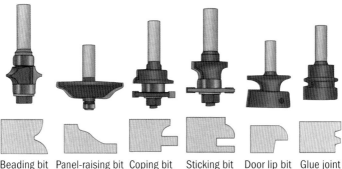

| Beading bit | Panel-raising bit | Coping bit (Rail cutter) | Sticking bit (Stile cutter) | Door lip bit | Glue joint bit |

MAKING MOLDINGS

Installed in a table-mounted router, this traditional molding bit can transform a plain board into an elaborate molding.

Routers and shapers are most often chosen to cut moldings, and the use of the table-mounted router for this purpose is shown on page 57.

Molding operations can be hazardous. The cutters strike with great force, and are capable of causing severe kickback and inflicting serious wounds.

Two principal safety rules apply to saws and routers. No single cut should be deeper than ⅛ inch; many shallow passes will produce superior results and reduce the risk of kickback. To ensure adequate control over your work, never mold stock that is shorter than 12 inches or narrower than 4 inches. If narrow molding is required, it can be ripped from wider stock when the shaping operation is complete.

SETTING UP A ROUTER TABLE

Mounting the router in the table

Install your router in a table following the manufacturer's instructions. For the model shown, loosen the clamp screw on the router base plate and remove the plate from the body of the tool. Unscrew the sub-base and fasten the base plate to the

Clamp screw

underside of the router table, aligning the predrilled holes in the plate with those in the table. Install a bit in the router, then screw the body of the tool into the base plate. Tighten the clamp screw *(right)*.

Adjusting the fence

Loosen the four adjustment screws and move the two halves of the fence as close as possible to the bit without touching the cutting edges. Tighten the screws, then set the width of cut, moving the fence back from the bit for a wide cut and advancing

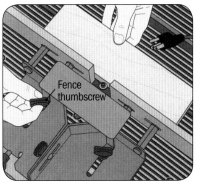

Fence thumbscrew

it for a shallow pass. For a cutting width equal to the diameter of the piloted panel-raising bit shown, loosen the four thumbscrews behind the fence. Then hold a straight board against the fence and move both halves together until the board contacts the pilot *(right)*. Tighten the thumbscrews.

ROUTING A MOLDING

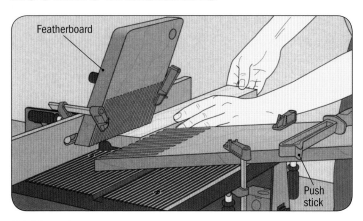

Featherboard

Push stick

Making the pass

To hold the workpiece in place, clamp two featherboards to the table as shown. Be sure to feed the stock into the cutter against the direction of bit rotation. With your workpiece clear of the bit, turn on the router and feed the stock into the cutting edge while holding it flush against the fence. To keep your hands safe, finish the pass with a push stick. Position the safety guard over the bit whenever possible.

ShopTip

A miter gauge for the router table
If your router table does not have a miter gauge slot, you can build a simple device to guide stock across the table while keeping it square to the fence. The jig consists of an L-shaped support piece and a guide that rides along the front edge of the table. To use the jig, butt the end of the workpiece against the fence while holding its edge against the support piece. Then push the workpiece and the gauge together into the bit.

MOLDING ON THE ROUTER TABLE

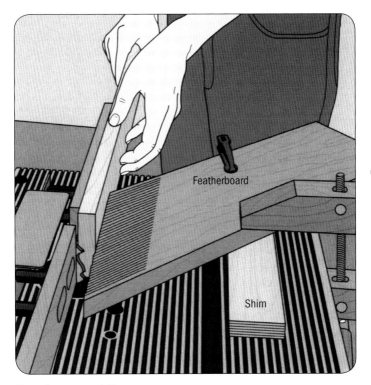

Featherboard

Shim

Routing a molding

Install a molding bit in your router and mount the tool in a table. If you are using a large bit, adjust the fence for a shallow cut—about ⅛ inch; do not attempt to rout the full profile in one pass. To hold the workpiece in place, clamp a featherboard to the table in line with the bit; raise the featherboard with a wood shim so that it supports the middle of the workpiece. With your stock clear of the bit, turn on the router and slowly feed the workpiece into the cutting edge while holding it flush against the fence *(above)*.

ROUTER TABLE MITER GAUGE

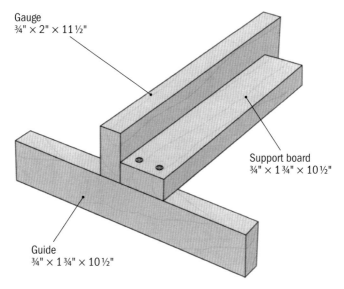

Gauge
¾" × 2" × 11½"

Support board
¾" × 1¾" × 10½"

Guide
¾" × 1¾" × 10½"

If you do not have a miter gauge or if your router table does not have a slot for one, use the shop-made jig shown above to guide stock accurately across the table. This device is especially helpful for keeping long, narrow boards perpendicular to the fence while cutting into their ends. Since the fence butts against the workpiece, the jig also helps to reduce tearout.

The dimensions of the jig will depend on the size of your table, but those suggested in the illustration are suitable for most commercial models. The length of the gauge—less the thickness of the guide—should not exceed the distance between the bit's pilot and the edge of the table.

ROUTER TABLE
MITER GAUGE *(continued)*

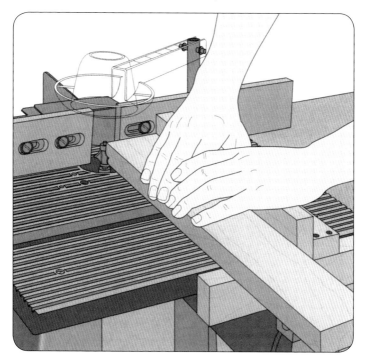

To assemble the jig, screw together the gauge and support board, making sure that they are aligned at one end. Countersink the screws into the face of the gauge. Then screw this assembly into the top edge of the guide.

To use the miter gauge, position it on the infeed side of the bit with the guide flush against the edge of the table. Then butt the end of the workpiece against the fence while holding its edge flush against the gauge. With the thumbs of both hands hooked over the jig, push the workpiece and the gauge together to make the cut *(above)*.

MAKING A STOPPED CUT ON A ROUTER TABLE

Bit position mark

Setting up the cut

Mark a cutting line on the face of the workpiece for the end of the cut.
Align the end of the stock with the cutting edge of the bit, then draw a
line on a strip of masking tape to mark the position of the cutter when it
is hidden by the workpiece *(above)*.

FEEDING THE STOCK

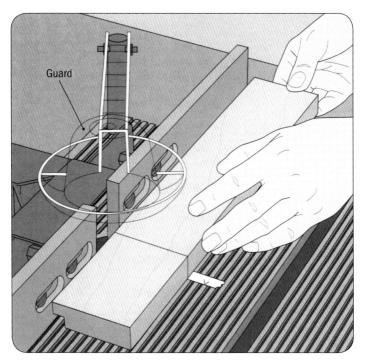

Guard

With the workpiece clear of the bit, position the guard and turn on the router. Press the stock flush against the fence while feeding it into the bit. Stop the cut once the cutting line of the workpiece meets the bit location mark *(above)*.

Although basic router techniques remain essentially unchanged no matter what the operation, cutting grooves involves special skills, whether the cuts are intended to be ornamental or functional.

This chapter demonstrates the tools and techniques used to rout a wide assortment of grooves, from the simple dadoes used to assemble carcases and cabinets to recesses for inlays and the graceful patterns that can form the decorative focus of a piece of furniture.

Many techniques will be used frequently, as the cuts are essential to most projects; others, although perhaps less commonly used, will allow you to extend the scope of your work and improve the level of your craftsmanship.

The best router to use depends on the task at hand. Although a standard router will perform virtually every job adequately,

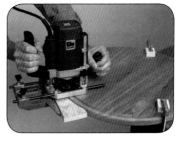

A core box bit carves a circular groove near the edge of a walnut tabletop. To ensure that this decorative cut follows the arc of the workpiece, a curved extension is fastened to a commercial edge guide to ride along the edge of the stock.

Fitted with a straight bit, a router cuts a dado for a shelf in a carcase side panel—with the help of a commercial edge guide.

a plunge router is preferred for interior cuts, such as routing stopped grooves *(page 100)* or cutting recesses for inlay *(page 128)*, since it allows you to align the bit over the cut and plunge it into the stock.

For safety and precision, it is often best to mount your router in a table *(page 112)*.

A router table affords a high degree of control that makes it a relatively simple task to rout stopped grooves and rabbets.

On page 126 we show techniques for following a predetermined pattern. Whether your router has plunging capabilities or not, and whether or not it is mounted in a table, you will be using a wide variety of accessories—jigs, bits, cutters, guides, and templates—that ease the completion of certain tasks and make others possible. A selection of commercial accessories is shown on page 95. Throughout this chapter you will find illustrated instructions for building your own accessories.

With these—and a little knowledge and imagination—you can make your router one of your most valuable tools.

A GALLERY OF GROOVES AND ACCESSORIES

Dadoes and Grooves

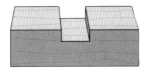

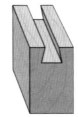

Dovetail groove
A wedge-shaped channel, typically interlocks with a mating board, forming part of a sliding dovetail joint.

Dado
A rectangular channel cut across the workpiece grain; typically forms part of a joint, but can also be used for decoration.

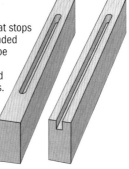

Blind groove
A cut along the grain that stops short of both ends; rounded ends left by router can be squared with a chisel. Used in both joinery and ornamental applications.

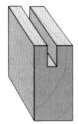

Groove
A cut along the grain of a workpiece, forming a rectangular channel; may be decorative but usually functional.

Stopped groove
A cut that stops short of one end.

Rabbet
A cut in the edge or end of a workpiece, with or across the grain.

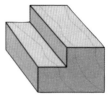

A GALLERY OF GROOVES
AND ACCESSORIES *(continued)*

Grooving Accessories

Straightedge guide
Model shown is self-
clamping; available
in various lengths.

Edge and circle guide
Edge guide holds router
a set distance from edge of
workpiece for straight cuts;
screw or pin inserted through
base of guide allows jig to pivot
around a centerpoint for cutting
circles. Adjustable guide rods
attach to router base plate.

Edge guide
Keeps router bit square to
board edges for grooving cuts.
Rods attach to router base
plate and fence rides along
workpiece edge. Fence can be
fitted with contoured shop-
made extension to help follow
edges of circular work.

ADJUSTABLE CIRCLE-CUTTING JIG

The shop-made jig shown below allows the router to cut circles of any diameter. Size the pieces of the jig to suit the job at hand. The center block can be cut from ¾-inch-thick stock; make it about 3 inches wide and 6 inches long. The diameter of the hardwood dowels depends on the size of the predrilled holes in the base plate of your router; cut the dowels longer than the radius of the largest circle you expect to rout.

To assemble the jig, slip the dowels into the holes in the router base plate, then set the tool flat on a work surface. Butt one edge of the center block against the ends of the dowels and mark the two points where the rods contact the edge. Bore a hole halfway through the block at each point, then spread a little glue in the holes and insert the dowels. Fix them in place with brads. Next, mark the center of the block and bore a hole through it for a screw.

To set up the cut, place your stock on the work surface. Butt wood scraps against the edges of the workpiece to act as cleats, then screw them in place. Mark the radius of the circle and its centerpoint. Install a straight bit in the router and set the cutting depth. For a deep cut, make several shallow passes.

ADJUSTABLE
CIRCLE-CUTTING JIG *(continued)*

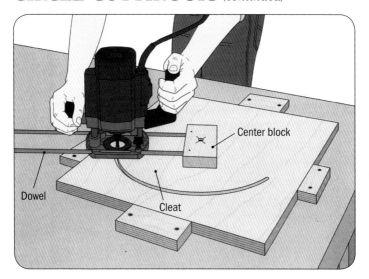

Center block

Dowel

Cleat

To use the jig, attach the block to the center of the circle and slide the dowels along the router base plate until the edge of the bit closest to the circle's center is aligned with the end of the marked radius. Tighten the screws in the base plate to hold the dowels in place. Then rout the circle, feeding the router in a clockwise direction *(above)*.

DADO CUTS

At one time, cutting dadoes cleanly and accurately was a painstaking task involving a specially designed hand plane or a saw and a wood chisel. Today, a router fitted with a straight bit can make quick work of any dado cut.

Whether you are routing a dado or a groove, the maximum depth of a single pass will depend on the hardness of the stock and the size of your router. In general, deep channels in

A straight bit carves a groove in a board. Riding an edge guide along the board produces a cut parallel to the edge.

hardwood require several passes. For cuts whose width exceeds the diameter of the bits you have on hand, make a series of passes. Three adjacent passes with a ½-inch bit, for example, will carve a dado or groove up to 1½ inches wide. (Usually, however, it would be better to make four slightly narrower cuts.)

The following pages display several useful dadoing jigs. For cuts close to the edge of a workpiece, the edge guide supplied with the router is a helpful tool, as shown in the photograph above. For cuts farther in from the edge, use a commercial or shop-built straightedge guide. As shown on page 100, stopped grooves are easy to cut using a straightedge and two stop blocks.

While any router will get the job done, a plunge router is best for making stopped dadoes and grooves. A standard router requires that you begin a stopped cut by tilting the base plate and pivoting the bit into the work; with a plunge router, you can hold the tool flat on the surface while plunging the bit straight into the wood.

CUTTING A GROOVE

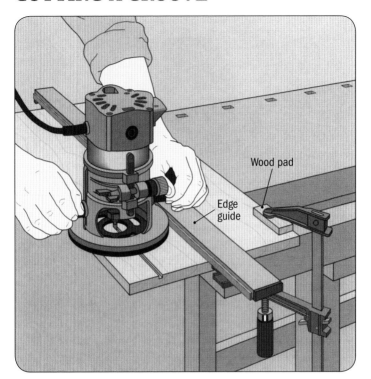

Wood pad

Edge
guide

Using an edge guide

Clamp your stock to a work surface, protecting the workpiece with wood
pads, then mark the beginning of the groove on the face of the stock.
Clamp an edge guide to the workpiece, using a tape measure to make
certain the guide is the same distance from the cutting mark as the gap
between the edge of the router base plate and the outermost part of the
bit. The guide must be parallel to the workpiece edge. With a firm grip
on the router, feed the bit into the stock at one end of the board, butting
the tool's base plate against the edge guide *(above)*.

ROUTING A STOPPED GROOVE

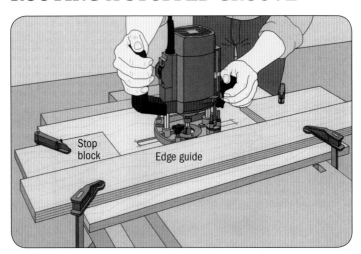

Stop block

Edge guide

Using an edge guide and stop blocks

Set the stock on a work surface, then center the bit over the cutting lines. Clamp an edge guide to the workpiece flush against the router base plate; check that the guide is parallel to the edge of the workpiece. Next align the bit with one end of the marked lines and clamp a stop block to the workpiece flush with the router base plate. Repeat the process at the other end of the groove. To start the cut, rest the base plate on the workpiece with the bit clear of the stock and the plate butted against the edge guide and one of the stop blocks. Then plunge the bit into the stock. Guide the router toward the other stop block, keeping the base plate flush against the edge guide *(above)*.

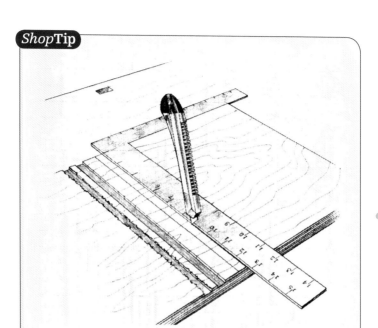

Preventing tearout

Cutting a dado in plywood can result in torn wood fibers along the edges of the cut.

To reduce tearout, score the outline of the dado with a utility knife. The incision will sever the wood fibers, keeping the edges of the dado clean.

ROUTING DADOES IN CARCASE SIDES

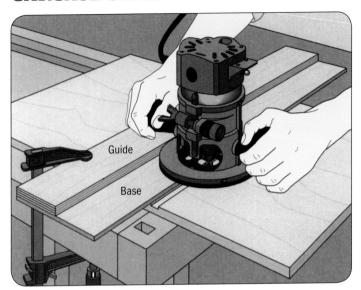

Guide

Base

Making and using an edge guide

Made from two pieces of plywood, the shop-built jig shown at left
enables you to make quick work of a dado cut. Since the distance
between the guide and the edge of the base is the same as the gap
between the edge of the router base plate and the bit, the jig can
be quickly lined up with the dado outline. Cut the base from ¼-inch
plywood and the guide from ¾-inch plywood; rip the pieces to widths
to suit your router set up. Screw the two pieces together, making sure
to countersink the fasteners. To rout the dado, set the stock on a work
surface and clamp the edge guide atop the workpiece, aligning the edge
of the jig base with the cutting marks. Set the router's cutting depth,
remembering to account for the thickness of the base. Rout the channel
(*above*), keeping the base flush against the guide and flat on the base.

CUTTING TWO DADOES IN ONE PASS

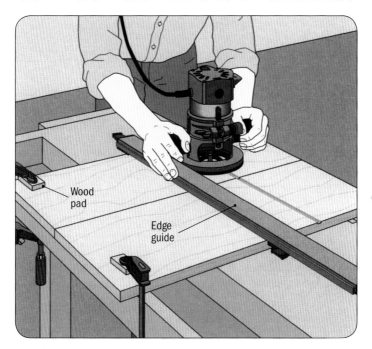

Wood pad

Edge guide

For a fixed shelf to sit level in a bookcase or cabinet, it must rest in dadoes at the same height in both side panels. One way to make certain the cuts line up is to rout both dadoes at the same time. Clamp the stock to a work surface, ensuring that the ends of the panels are aligned; protect the workpieces with wood pads. Then clamp an edge guide to the stock, positioning the jig so the router bit will line up directly over the dado outline. Make certain that the edge guide is square to the panel edges. Rout the dado *(above)*.

T-SQUARE JIG FOR GROOVING

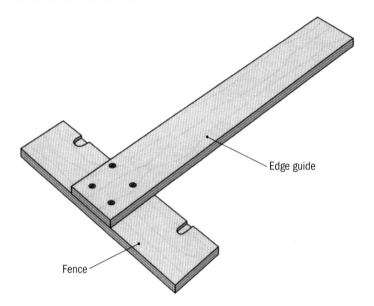

Edge guide

Fence

To rout dadoes and grooves that are straight and perfectly square to the edge of your stock, construct a T-square jig like the one shown at right, made from ¾-inch plywood.

Size the jig to accommodate the stock you will be using and the diameter of your router base plate. Make the edge guide about 4 inches wide and at least as long as the width of the workpiece; the fence, also about 4 inches wide, should extend on either side of the guide by about the width of the router base plate.

To assemble the jig, screw the fence to the edge guide with countersunk screws. Use a try square to make certain the two pieces are perpendicular to each other. Then clamp the jig to a work surface and rout

T-SQUARE JIG
FOR GROOVING *(continued)*

a short dado on each side of the fence, using your two most commonly used bits—often ½- and ¾-inch. These dadoes in the fence will minimize tearout when the jig is used, as well as serving to align the jig.

To use the jig, clamp it to the workpiece, aligning the appropriate dado in the fence with the outline on the stock. When making the cut, keep the router base plate firmly against the edge guide *(above)*. Continue the cut a short distance into the fence before stopping the router.

QUICK-SETUP GROOVING JIG

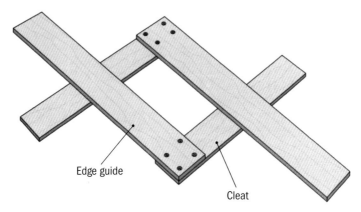

Edge guide

Cleat

Consisting of four strips of ¾-inch plywood assembled to form two Ls, the jig shown above makes it easy to rout dadoes and grooves with minimal tearout. Make all the pieces of the jig about 4 inches wide. Cut the edge guides a few inches longer than the cut you intend to make. The cleats should be long enough to overlap the adjacent edge guide by several inches when the jig is set up. Attach the cleats to the edge guides, making sure that the pieces are perpendicular to each other; use four countersunk screws for each connection.

Set up the jig by clamping the stock to a work surface and butting the cleats against the workpiece at the beginning and end of the cut. Then set your router between the edge guides, aligning the bit over the dado outline. Slide the guides together until they butt against each side of the router base plate. Secure the jig by clamping it at opposing corners and to the workpiece. Then turn on the router and, with the

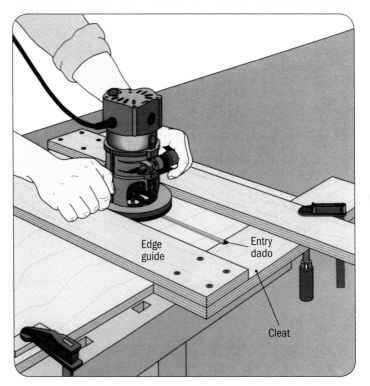

Edge guide

Entry dado

Cleat

tool between the edge guides, start the cut in the cleat, creating an entry dado. Guide the router across the workpiece *(above)*, extending the cut completely through the stock and into the second cleat. This will minimize tearout as the bit exits the workpiece. If you need to rout several dadoes of the same size, leave the jig clamped together and align the entry dado with the cutting lines marked on the stock.

CUTTING GROOVES IN THIN STOCK

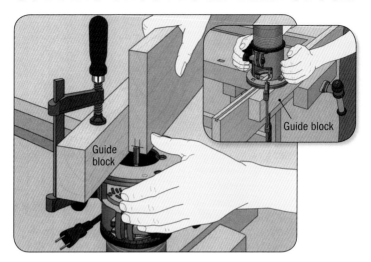

Guide block

Guide block

Grooving a narrow edge

To rout a groove along a surface that is too narrow to accommodate an edge guide, attach a short guide block to the router itself. Install a straight bit and set the router upside down on a work surface. Remove the sub-base if necessary and screw the guide block to the tool through one of the predrilled holes in the base plate. Mark the width of the groove on one end of the workpiece and align the marks with the bit. Then pivot the guide block until it is flush against the face of the stock. Clamp the guide to the base plate. Hold the marked end of the workpiece against the bit again to check that the guide is positioned properly *(above, left)*. To cut the groove, secure the workpiece edge up in a vise. Set the router flat on the edge of the board with the bit clear of the stock at one end and the guide block flush against the face of the workpiece. As you feed the bit through the cut, keep the base plate flat on the board's edge and the guide block pressed against the workpiece *(above, right)*. Reposition the board, if necessary, to avoid hitting the vise with the clamp.

*Shop*Tip

Eliminating tearout

Routers have a tendency to cause tearout, particularly as they exit a workpiece at the end of a dado cut. To minimize splintering, always use an edge guide for straight cuts and secure a wood block the same thickness as your workpiece along the edge from which the bit will emerge. The pressure of the block against the workpiece will help to eliminate tearout.

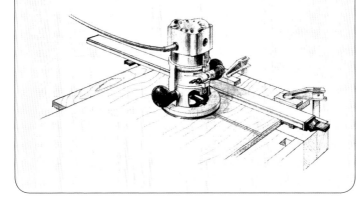

ADJUSTABLE DADO JIG

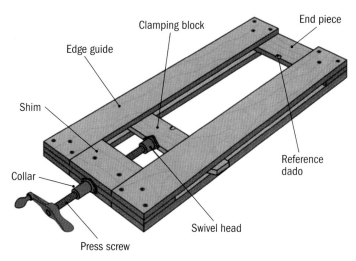

The jig shown at right is ideal if you do much routing of dadoes in carcase panels. The jig features edge guides to keep the cut perpendicular to the edges of the workpiece and a sliding clamping block to hold the panel securely. Size the pieces so the distance between the edge guides equals the diameter of your router's base plate. The guides should be long enough to allow you to clamp the widest panel you plan to cut.

Cut the four guide pieces, the two ends, and shims from ¾-inch plywood; make all the pieces 4 inches wide. Assemble the end and guide pieces so the router base plate is flush against the guides along their entire length. Then screw the pieces together, sandwiching the end pieces between the guides. At one end of the frame, attach shims to the top and bottom of the end piece. Countersink all your fasteners. Cut the clamping block from ¾-inch-thick stock; make it about 3 inches wide and long enough to slide between the edge guides. To install the

ADJUSTABLE DADO JIG *(continued)*

press screw, bore a hole for the threads through the shimmed end piece. Remove the swivel head from the press screw and fasten it to the middle of the clamping block. Attach the threaded section to the swivel head and screw the collar to the end piece. Use the router to cut short reference dadoes in the other end piece and the clamping block.

To use the jig, slide the workpiece between the edge guides, aligning the cutting lines with the reference dadoes. Secure the panel in position with the press screw. Clamp the jig to a work surface. With the bit clear of the work, turn on the router and start the cut at the reference dado in the end piece, making certain the router is between the edge guides. Feed the bit into the workpiece, keeping the base plate flat on the stock *(above)*. To minimize tearout, only raise the router clear of the work once the bit exits the workpiece and reaches the reference dado in the clamping block.

GROOVING ON A ROUTER TABLE

Mounted upside down in a table, the router works very much like a shaper. In addition to carving decorative contours on board edges and making precise joinery cuts, a table-mounted router offers a safe and quick method to cut dadoes and grooves. The setup allows you to exert greater control over routing operations.

Virtually any dadoing operation can be performed with a table-mounted router, but the arrangement is particularly

A table-mounted router fitted with a piloted three-wing slotting cutter routs a groove along the inside of a drawer for a bottom panel. Keeping the pilot against the stock keeps the groove depth uniform and controls kickback.

convenient for cutting grooves in narrow stock (*opposite*). Stopped grooves can be cut with either a straight bit or a three-wing slotting cutter. Your best choice is the slotting cutter since it allows the workpiece to be pivoted into the cutter with the face of the board flat on the table. With a straight bit, the stock is lowered onto the bit edge down, with the board face resting against the fence—a trickier operation.

Remember that several light cuts are safer and more accurate than one heavy pass. If you need to cut a groove wider than your largest straight bit, make two or more passes, advancing the fence after each pass. For deep grooves, also make a series of cuts, increasing the cutting depth for each pass.

CUTTING A GROOVE IN A BOARD EDGE

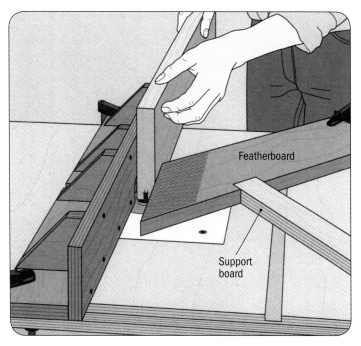

Featherboard

Support board

Making the cut

With a straight bit in the router, set the cutting depth and align the cutting marks with the bit. For the shop-built router table and clamp-on fence shown in the illustration, position the fence flush against the board face and secure it to the tabletop; make certain the fence is parallel to the edge of the table. To secure the workpiece, clamp a featherboard to the table opposite the bit; clamp a support board at a 90° angle to the featherboard for extra pressure. Feed the workpiece into the bit, pressing the stock firmly against the fence *(above)*. If you are working with narrow stock, protect your fingers from the bit by using a push stick.

CUTTING A STOPPED GROOVE

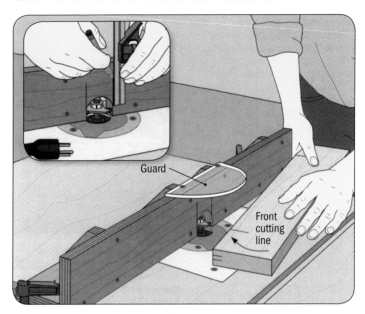

Guard

Front
cutting
line

Setting up and starting the cut

Mount your router in a table with a three-wing slotting cutter in the tool.
Mark two sets of cutting lines on the workpiece: one on its leading end for
the width and position of the groove and the other on its face for the length
of the groove. Butt the marks on the end of the board against the cutter
and adjust the cutter height. Install the fence on the table, lining it up with
the pilot on the cutter. To help you determine the location of the cutter when
it is hidden by the workpiece during this cut, mark the points on the fence
where the bit starts and stops cutting *(inset)*. Attach the guard to the fence.
To start the cut, turn on the router with the workpiece clear of the bit. Hold
the board face down on the table and align the front cutting line on the
workpiece with the bit cutting mark on the fence farthest from you. Slowly
pivot the board into the cutter *(above)*.

FINISHING THE CUT

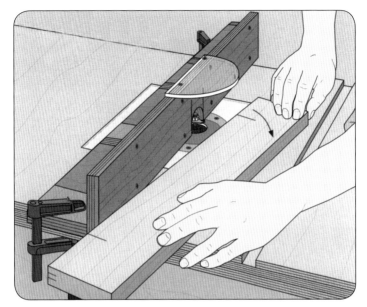

When the workpiece is flush against the fence, feed it forward while pressing it down and against the fence. Continue the cut until the back cutting line on the workpiece aligns with the bit cutting mark closest to you. Pivot the trailing end of the workpiece away from the cutter with your right hand *(above)*, steadying the board against the table and fence by hooking your left hand around the edge of the table. Avoid lifting the board until the stock is clear of the cutter. Use a chisel to square the ends of the groove, if necessary.

RABBETS

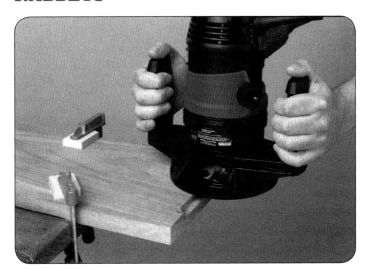

A rabbeting bit carves a stopped rabbet into the underside of a shelf. The rabbet will fit into a wooden shelf support attached to the side of a carcase. This technique conceals both the rabbet and the shelf support.

A rabbet is one of the most basic of cuts, commonly used in a corner joint or to accommodate the back of a cabinet. A rabbet can be routed with a piloted rabbeting bit or a straight bit in conjunction with an edge guide.

With a piloted bit, the pilot bearing rides along the edge of the workpiece while the cutting edges above the bearing rout the stock. The width of the rabbet is equal to one-half the difference between the diameter of the bit and the diameter of the bearing. A 1¼-inch-diameter bit with a ½-inch bearing, for example, will cut a rabbet ⅜ inch wide. Many router bit manufacturers now sell rabbeting sets, consisting of a single cutter and a selection of different-sized bearings.

A straight bit and an edge guide can be used to cut rabbets of any width. To rout extra-wide rabbets that exceed the capacity of your largest bit, make two or more passes, adjusting the location of the edge guide each time.

CUTTING A RABBET

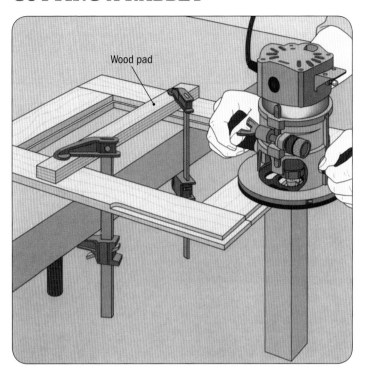

Wood pad

Using a piloted bit

Clamp your stock to a work surface; for the door frame shown, about one-half of the workpiece should extend beyond the table's edge. Gripping the router firmly with both hands, butt its base plate on the workpiece and guide the bit into the stock; make sure the cutting edge is clear of the table. Keeping the pilot bearing pressed against the edge of the workpiece, feed the bit around the perimeter of the frame in a counterclockwise direction *(above)*. Once the bit nears the table on the other side of the workpiece, stop the cut and turn off the router. Loosen the clamps, rotate the workpiece, and clamp it again. Follow the same routing procedures to complete the operation.

RABBETING JIG

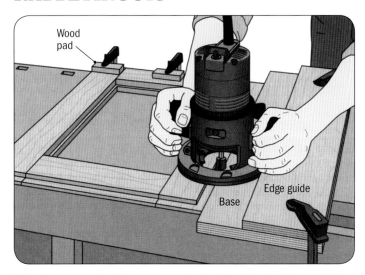

Make it easy to cut wide or non-standard-width rabbets with a straight bit and the simple jig shown at right. Made from two strips of wood, the jig is simple to assemble and set up.

Cut the base from plywood or solid stock the same thickness as your workpiece. Make the edge guide from ¾-inch plywood. Both pieces should be at least as long as the largest piece you plan to cut.

To set up the jig, secure the stock to a work surface and outline the rabbet on it. Butt the jig base against the edge of the stock. Align the bit over the cutting mark, then position the edge guide flush against the router base plate. Fasten the edge guide to the base of the jig with countersunk screws, ensuring that both boards are parallel to the edge of the workpiece. Clamp the jig in position. In making the cut, feed the bit against the direction of bit rotation and keep the tool's base plate pressed firmly against the edge guide throughout the operation.

ShopTip

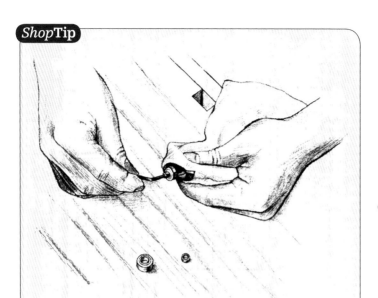

Cutting rabbets of different widths
Instead of stocking several bits of different diameters, you can
buy a rabbeting kit, consisting of a single cutter and a set of
pilot bearings of various sizes. A typical kit allows you to cut
rabbets ranging in width from ¼ to ⁷⁄₁₆ inch. Use a hex wrench
to install the appropriate bearing for the rabbet you wish to cut.
If you already own a piloted rabbeting bit, you can still benefit
from this convenience by buying the bearings separately.

CIRCULAR GROOVES

A router cuts a decorative groove in a tabletop with the help of a commercial circle guide. Fixed to the stock with a screw, the jig pivots around the center of the circle. The screw hole can be concealed later with a wood plug.

The router is one of the few tools that excel at making both curved and straight cuts with equal ease. Assisted by a guide or jig that maintains the distance between the bit and the center of the circle, the router can cut decorative curves and circles with unerring precision. One of the many styles of commercial guides available is shown in the photo above, but the circle and edge guide supplied with the router is usually adequate for the task. Rather than pivoting around a fixed point at a circle's center, this guide follows the edge of the workpiece and is useful only when the circular cut is concentric with the circumference of the workpiece.

While commercial jigs can be adjusted to cut circles of varying diameters, some guides are too short to cut larger arcs. A shop-made jig like that described on page 96 will solve this problem.

As with cutting dadoes, a plunge router is more convenient than a standard tool for routing circles. And remember, for safety's sake and to reduce tearout, cut deep grooves with several passes, rather than in one cut.

ROUTING A CIRCLE

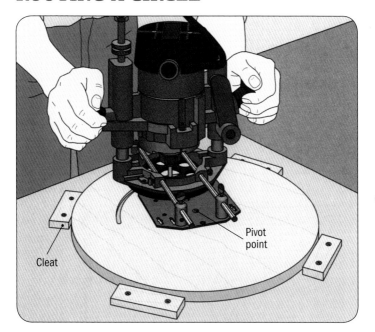

Pivot point

Cleat

Using a plunge router

Butt wood scraps as cleats against the edges of the workpiece and screw them in place. Install a straight bit in the router, then mark the location of the groove and the center of the circle. Use a screw or the fulcrum pin provided with a commercial circle-cutting guide to fix the pivot point of the jig to the center of the circle; the guide should be secure, but able to pivot. Install the router on the guide so the bit is aligned with the groove mark. With the cutter clear of the workpiece, grip the router firmly and plunge the bit into the stock. Feed the tool steadily in a clockwise direction *(above)* until the circle is completed.

COMPASS JIG

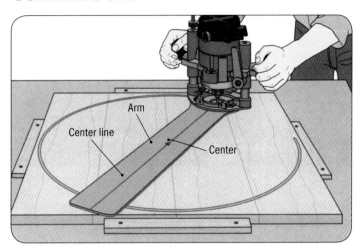

To cut larger circles than most commercial circle-cutting guides allow, use the compass jig shown below. Make the device from ¼-inch hardboard, sizing the jig to suit your router and the radius of the largest circle you plan to cut. Cut the router-end of the jig in the shape of a circle about the size of your tool's base plate.

The arm of the jig should be at least 2 inches wide and longer than the radius of the circle you will be cutting. Cut out the jig with a band saw or a saber saw, then bore a hole in the center of the rounded end to accommodate the router bit. To mount the jig on your router, remove the sub-base and set the tool on the circular part of the jig. With the bit centered over the hole, mark the locations of the predrilled holes in the base plate. Bore the holes and screw the jig to the router. Finally, draw a line down the center of the jig arm.

COMPASS JIG *(continued)*

To use the jig, determine the radius of the circle you wish to cut and transfer this length to the jig, measuring from the edge of the bit closest to the center of the circle along the center line. Bore a hole at the center mark, then screw the jig to the workpiece. Secure the stock to a work surface with cleats. Rout the circle as you would with a commercial guide, guiding the router in a clockwise direction.

ShopTip

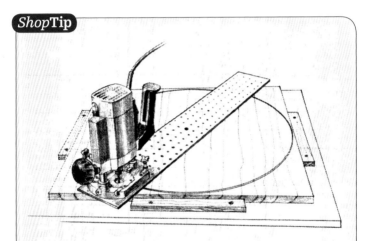

Quick compass jig
Use a strip of perforated hardboard cut slightly wider than the router base plate to fabricate a simple shop-made circle-cutting jig for your tool. Cut the strip so that one row of holes runs down the center of the jig. Use the jig as described above, but attach it to your router and the workpiece through the hardboard's existing perforations.

USING A STANDARD ROUTER

Template

Set up your stock and router as you would for working with a plunge router. With the tool on the template, tilt it so the bit is clear of the stock, but aligned over the marked outline. Gripping the router firmly, turn it on and lower the cutter into the workpiece until the base plate is flat on the surface and the template guide is butted against the edge of the template *(above)*. Feed the bit in a clockwise direction until the cut is finished; ride the guide along the template throughout the operation.

CUTTING A HINGE MORTISE

Using a template

Pattern routing is an excellent method for cutting mortises for hinges. Install a straight bit and a template guide in your router. Then make the template from a piece of ¾-inch plywood that is wide enough to support the router. Outline the hinge leaf on the template, being sure to compensate for the template guide and the thickness of the fence, which is also made from ¾-inch plywood. Cut out the template, then attach the fence with countersunk screws *(top)*. To use the jig, secure the door edge up, mark the hinge outline on the workpiece, and clamp the template in position, aligning the cut-out with the outline on the door edge and butting the fence against the face of

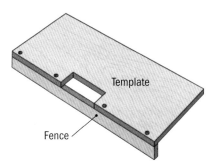

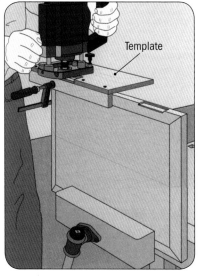

the door. Make the cut *(bottom)*, moving the router in small clockwise circles until the bottom of the recess is smooth, then square the corners with a wood chisel.

ADJUSTABLE ROUTING GUIDE

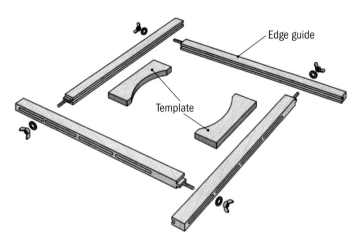

Edge guide

Template

The jig shown above is ideal for routing rectangular grooves and it can be fitted with templates for curved cuts. The jig can be adjusted to a wide range of sizes and proportions.

Cut the four guides from 1-by-2 stock, making them long enough to accommodate the largest workpiece you plan to handle. The guides are assembled using a combination of grooves, tenons, mortises, and hanger bolts. Rout a continuous groove—3/8 inch deep and wide—along the inside edge of each guide. Then cut a two-shouldered tenon at one end of each guide; size the tenon to fit in the groove. Bore a pilot hole into the middle of each tenon for a 3/8-inch-diameter hanger bolt. Screw the bolts in place, leaving enough thread protruding to feed the bolt through the adjacent edge guide and slip on a washer and wing nut. Finally, rout 3/8-inch-wide mortises through the guides; starting about 3½ inches from each end, make the cuts 4 inches long, separated by about ½ inch of solid wood. Assemble the jig by slipping the tenons and hanger bolts through the grooves and mortises of the adjacent guide

ADJUSTABLE ROUTING
GUIDE *(continued)*

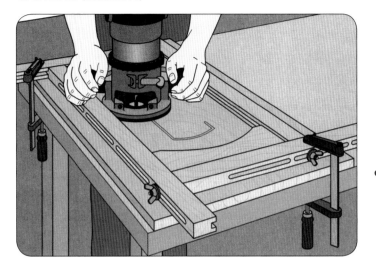

and installing the washers and nuts. To produce a curved pattern, you will also need to make templates like the ones in the illustration to guide the router along the contours; use double-sided tape to secure the templates to the workpiece.

To use the jig, set your stock on a work surface and outline the pattern on the surface. Loosen the wing nuts of the jig, then position it on the stock so the edge guides frame the outline. Place the router flat on the workpiece and align the bit with one edge of the outline. Butt one of the edge guides flush against the router base plate. Repeat on the other edges until all four guides and any templates for curved cuts are in position. Tighten the wing nuts, reposition the jig on the workpiece, and clamp it in place. Plunge the bit into the stock and make the cut in a clockwise direction, keeping the base plate flush against an edge guide or template at all times. For repeat cuts, simply clamp the jig to the new workpiece and rout the pattern *(above)*.

INLAYING

A marquetry inlay, formed from a pattern of dyed wood set in a veneer, graces a mahogany board. The inlay was glued into a routed recess.

Inlaying is the decorative process of setting a thin strip of wood into a recess cut in the surface of a workpiece. A wide range of inlays is available, from simple bands of exotic wood to elaborate marquetry motifs consisting of several veneers assembled into an attractive design. An example of the latter is shown below. Before the development of the router, recesses for inlays used to be cut with a wood chisel or a router plane—a laborious, time-consuming task. A router fitted with a straight bit can complete this chore quickly and precisely. Still, it is an exacting task because the depression must match the inlay precisely. Following the steps presented below and opposite will help you achieve good results. With edge guides to confine the router's movements, you can be assured of a perfect match between the size of the recess and the dimensions of the inlay.

Recesses for marquetry inlay should be as deep or slightly deeper than the thickness of the inlay, typically $\frac{1}{20}$ inch. If the inlay is slightly recessed after the glue has dried, carefully sand the wood surrounding the inlay until the two surfaces are flush. If you are using solid wood inlay—thicker than marquetry—make the recess slightly shallower than the inlay's thickness, and sand the two surfaces even after glue-up. Spread a very thin layer of glue to secure the inlay in place. One final tip: Before plowing the recess, score its outline with a chisel or knife to avoid tearout along the edges.

SETTING A MARQUETRY INLAY IN PLACE

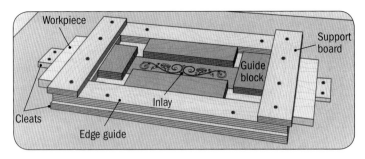

- Workpiece
- Support board
- Guide block
- Inlay
- Cleats
- Edge guide

Setting up the edge guides

After you set your stock on a work surface, butt wood scraps against the edges as cleats and screw them in place. Position the inlay and outline its edges on the surface. Then cut a strip of ¾-inch plywood so its width equals the distance between the edge of your router's base plate and its bit. Saw the strip into four pieces and butt them against the edges of the inlay to serve as guide blocks. Then rest four more plywood pieces against the guide blocks as edge guides. To keep the guides from moving, screw them to the cleats; in cases where this would involve screwing directly into the workpiece, such as at the ends of the workpiece shown, fasten support boards to the guides, then screw the boards to the guides that are already fixed in place *(above)*. Remove the inlay and guide blocks. Riding your router base plate against the edge guides ensures the recess will fit the inlay exactly.

ROUTING THE RECESS

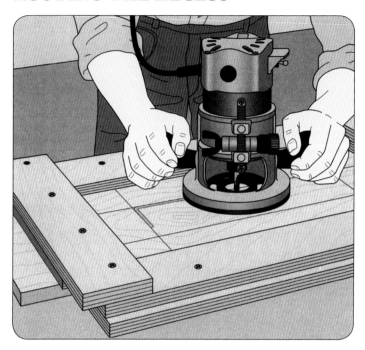

Set the router's cutting depth. Make a test cut in a scrap board and test-fit the inlay; adjust the cutting depth, if necessary. To make the cut, rest the router on the workpiece with the bit clear of the stock and above the outline. Then turn on the router and plunge the bit into the work-piece. Guide the tool in a clockwise direction to cut the outside edges of the recess, keeping the base plate flush against an edge guide at all times *(above)*. To complete the recess, rout out the remaining waste, feeding the tool against the direction of bit rotation as much as possible. Use a chisel to square the corners.

GLUING UP THE INLAY

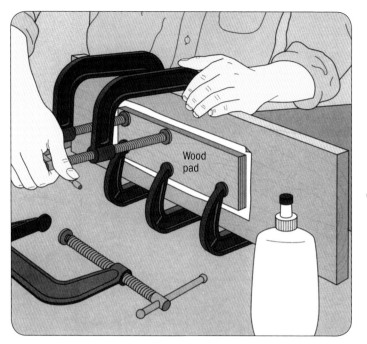

Once the recess is completed, cut a wood pad slightly smaller than the recess to hold the inlay in place. Spread a thin layer of glue in the recess and position the inlay in place, paper-side-up. Lay a piece of wax paper over the inlay to prevent the wood pad from bonding to it. Then set the pad in place. Use as many C clamps as necessary to distribute the clamping pressure evenly. Starting about 1 inch from the ends of the wood pad, space the clamps at 3- to 4-inch intervals; focus the pressure on the top half of the pad. Tighten the clamps just enough to hold the pad in place, then turn the workpiece over so that the first row of clamps is resting on the work surface. Install the second row of clamps along the other edge of the pad *(above)*. Finish tightening all of the clamps firmly.

CHAPTER 4:

Router Joinery

The router's ability to plunge into wood and cut precise, clean, straight-edged grooves makes it an excellent tool for the demanding task of joinery. Equipped with a battery of specially designed bits, jigs, and other accessories, the router can cut dozens of joints, ranging from the utilitarian rabbet to the most elaborate of dovetails. A dozen of these joints are presented on page 134. The remaining pages of the chapter provide step-by-step instructions for fashioning the cuts.

The mortise-and-tenon is the most popular method of assembling the frame in frame-and-panel construction. Many commercial jigs are available to help you cut this joint with a router. Some are essentially positioning jigs for centering the router bit on the edge of a workpiece (page 136). Other models are used to cut the joints for the rails and stiles of a frame (page 142). Shop-built

Paired with a multi-joint jig, a router makes quick work of carving the pins of a dovetail joint.

For a seamless fit, a long, interlocking joint like the tongue-and-groove calls for precision cutting. Here, the groove half of the joint is plowed on a router table by a three-wing slotting cutter.

jigs for routing mortises *(page 153)* and tenons *(page 155)* can also be made inexpensively. Another common frame-and-panel joint—the cope-and-stick *(page 156)*—offers strength and a decorative flourish.

Dovetail joints are best cut with the help of a variety of commercial jigs. Whether you cut the half-blind variety *(page 165)*, a common drawer joint, or the traditional through dovetail *(page 166)*, these jigs will help you produce the joint with unerring precision.

Joints can be either functional or decorative—or both. The sliding dovetail *(page 170)* and glue joint *(page 178)*, for example, are strong joints that remain invisible once they are assembled. The dovetail spline *(page 174)*, on the other hand, is primarily a visual detail.

Some joints, perhaps because they require long or repetitive cuts, are best produced on the router table. The box joint *(page 180)* and tongue-and-groove *(page 188)* are good examples.

ROUTER-MADE JOINTS

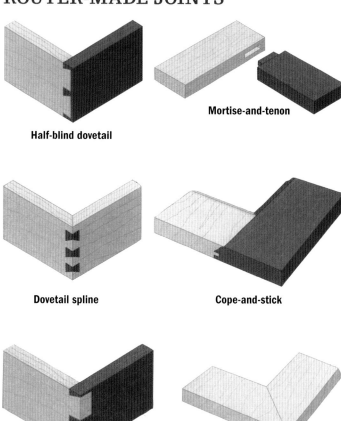

Half-blind dovetail

Mortise-and-tenon

Dovetail spline

Cope-and-stick

Through dovetail

Miter-and-spline

ROUTER-MADE JOINTS *(continued)*

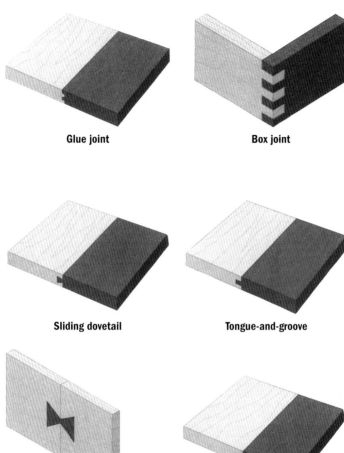

Glue joint

Box joint

Sliding dovetail

Tongue-and-groove

Butterfly key

Rule joint

ROUTER JOINERY JIGS

Mortise-and tenon jig
Used with router to cut matching mortises and tenons; jig is secured in vise and workpiece is then clamped to jig.

Size and built-in precision make a stationary joint-maker ideal for cutting various joints at production-line speed. The model shown features an adjustable table that moves back and forth and side to side, enhancing the machine's versatility.

Mortising jig
Attaches to router base plate to rout mortises; guide pins are positioned against board faces or edges, centering mortise in edge or face.

Interchangeable-template jig
Depending on template used, allows router to cut dovetail and box joints with a single setup; comes with guide bushing and router bits.

ROUTER JOINERY JIGS *(continued)*

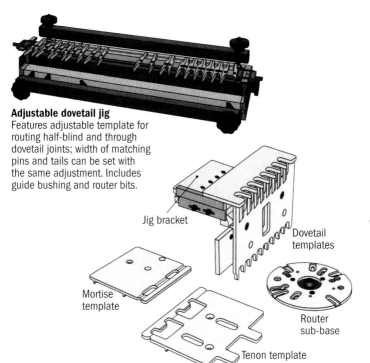

Adjustable dovetail jig
Features adjustable template for
routing half-blind and through
dovetail joints; width of matching
pins and tails can be set with
the same adjustment. Includes
guide bushing and router bits.

Jig bracket

Dovetail
templates

Mortise
template

Router
sub-base

Tenon template

Multi-joint jig
Used with router to cut dovetail,
box, finger, and mortise-and-
tenon joints. L-shaped bracket
is fastened to backup board
and secured in vise; appropriate
template is attached to bracket.
Comes with guide bushing,
router sub-base, and bits.

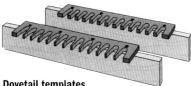

Dovetail templates
A set of two fixed templates fastened to
backup boards to rout through dovetail
joints; one template is for pins and
the other for tails. Various models are
available for routing different-size pins.
Comes with two piloted router bits.

DOUBLE DADO JOINT

The double dado joint connects two dadoes, one dado on the inside face of one board and the other dado—with one tongue shortened—on the end of the mating piece. The joint is stronger than a standard through dado because it provides more gluing surface. It is an ideal choice for joining boards of different thicknesses, such as attaching a drawer front to the sides, and provides good resistance to tension and racking. The setup shown in the steps below and on the following page will join a ¾-inch-thick drawer front to a ½-inch-thick drawer side. The three cuts can all be made with the same bit—a three-wing slotting cutter. In this case, a ¼-inch bit is used; the shim attached to the auxiliary fence is also ¼ inch thick. By varying the sizes of the cutter and shim, you can cut the same joint in boards of different thicknesses.

ROUTING A DOUBLE DADO JOINT

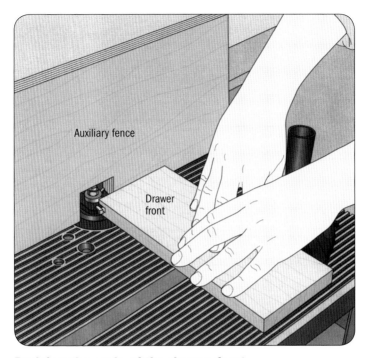

Dadoing the ends of the drawer front

If you are using double dadoes to assemble a drawer, cut the dadoes with
the shortened tongue on the ends of the drawer front. Start by installing a
three-wing slotting cutter in a router and mounting the tool in a table. Cut a
notch for the bit through an 8-inch-high auxiliary fence and attach the fence
in place; the high fence is essential for feeding stock across the table on
end. Position the fence in line with the outer edge of the bit pilot bearing and
parallel to the miter slot, then set the cutting height by butting the workpiece
against the bit and centering the cutter on the end of the board. Keeping the
face of the board flat on the table and the end pressed against the fence,
feed it into the cutter using the miter gauge *(above)*.

DADOING THE DRAWER SIDE

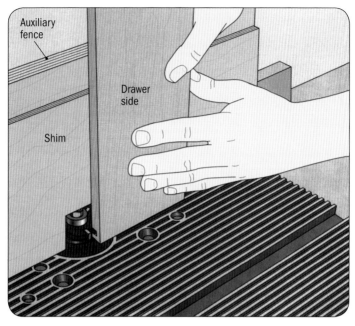

Cut a notch in a wood shim for the cutter and screw it to the auxiliary fence. The shim should be as long as the fence and equal in thickness to the difference in thickness between the drawer front and sides. To rout the dado in the drawer side, hold its end flat on the table and its inside face flush against the shim as you feed it across the table *(above)*. Be sure to keep your hands clear of the cutter.

TRIMMING THE INSIDE TONGUES ON THE DRAWER FRONT

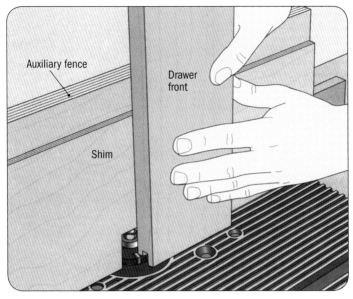

Auxiliary fence

Drawer front

Shim

To complete the joint, you need to shorten the inside tongue of each dado you routed earlier. Lower the cutting height of the bit so the bottom edge of the cutter is just above the tabletop. Then feed the drawer front across the table, holding the inside face against the shim *(above)*.

CORNER HALF-LAP JOINT

The corner half-lap joint is often used to assemble frames and doors. Adding dowels or screws to the joint provides an extra measure of strength. The joint can be cut on a table saw with a dado blade, but a router will do the job just as well. Do not try to make the cut freehand. This joint depends upon perfectly square shoulder cuts. Use a T-square like the one shown at right to guide the router.

ROUTING A CORNER HALF-LAP JOINT

Using a T-square jig

To rout half-laps with shoulders that are straight and square to the edges of the stock, use a T-square jig like the one shown at right. Make the jig from ¾-inch plywood so that each piece is about 4 inches wide; the fence should extend on either side of the edge

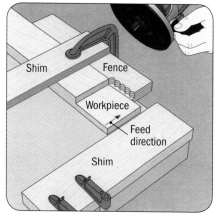

guide by about the width of the router base plate. Assemble the jig by attaching the fence to the guide with countersunk screws, using a try square to make certain the two pieces are perpendicular to each other. Mark the shoulder of the half-lap on your workpiece and set the stock on a work surface. Install a straight bit in the router, align the cutter with the shoulder line of the half-lap, and clamp the jig atop the workpiece so the edge guide is butted against the router base plate, and the edges of the fence and workpiece are flush against each other. Rout the half-lap with a series of passes that run across the end of the stock, as shown by the arrow in the illustration. Start at the end of the workpiece and continue until you make the last pass with the router riding along the edge guide.

CORNER HALF-LAP JOINT JIG

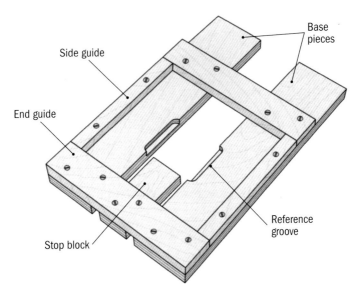

Base pieces

Side guide

End guide

Reference groove

Stop block

If you have to make corner half-laps in several boards of the same size, it is worth taking the time to build the jig at right. Cut the two base pieces and the stop block from plywood that is the same thickness as your stock. The base pieces should be wide enough to support the router base plate as you cut the half-laps and mount the side and end guides. Use solid wood strips for the four edge guides.

To assemble the jig, mark the shoulder of the half-lap on one workpiece and set the board face-up on a work surface. Butt the base pieces against the edges of the board so the shoulder mark is near the middle of the base pieces. Install a straight bit in the router and align the cutter with the shoulder mark. Position one end guide across the base pieces and against the tool's base plate. Without moving the workpiece, repeat the procedure to position the opposite guide. Now align the bit with the edges of the workpiece and attach the side guides,

CORNER HALF-LAP
JOINT JIG *(continued)*

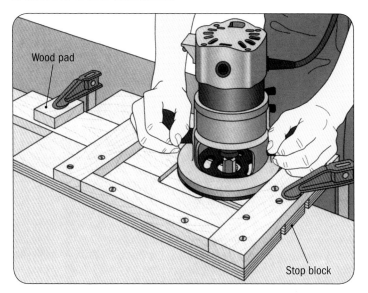

Wood pad

Stop block

leaving a slight gap between the router base plate and each guide. (The first half-lap you make with the jig will rout reference grooves in the base pieces.) Slip the stop block under the end guide, butt it against the end of the workpiece, and screw it in place. Countersink all fasteners.

To use the jig, clamp it to the work surface and slide the workpiece between the base pieces until it butts against the stop block. Protecting the stock with a wood pad, clamp the workpiece in place. Adjust the router's cutting depth to one-half the stock thickness. Then, with the router positioned inside the guides, grip the tool firmly, turn it on, and lower the bit into the workpiece. Guide the router in a clockwise direction to cut the outside edges of the half-lap, keeping the base plate flush against a guide at all times. Then rout out the remaining waste *(above)*, feeding the tool against the direction of bit rotation.

LOCK MITER JOINT

Also known as a drawer lock joint, the lock miter is often used to assemble drawers. The joint features identical cuts in the mating boards, one in a board end and the other along the joining face. Both cuts are produced on a router table with the same bit. Because the lock miter is suitable with plywood, it is a good alternative to dovetails in such situations.

ROUTING A LOCK MITER

Making the cuts

Install a lock miter bit in your router and mount the tool in a table. Attach a notched auxiliary fence and screw an extension board to the miter gauge. Set the bit height so the uppermost cutter is centered on the board end with the workpiece flat on the table. Position the fence so the bit will dado the stock without shortening it. Holding the workpiece against the fence and the miter gauge extension, feed the stock into the bit *(top)*. To cut the mating piece, clamp a guide block to it to ride along the top of the fence. Then feed the board on end into the cutter, keeping it flush against the fence with one hand while pushing it and the guide block forward with the other hand *(bottom)*.

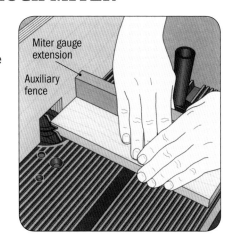

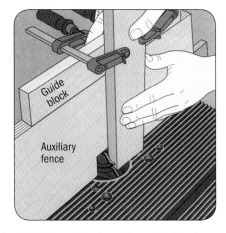

MORTISE-AND-TENON JOINTS

With origins in woodworking that date back more than 3,000 years, the mortise-and-tenon is a strong and versatile joint. There are many variations, but the basic principle is constant: a projecting tenon fits snugly into a mortise. The type shown here is the blind mortise-and-tenon joint.

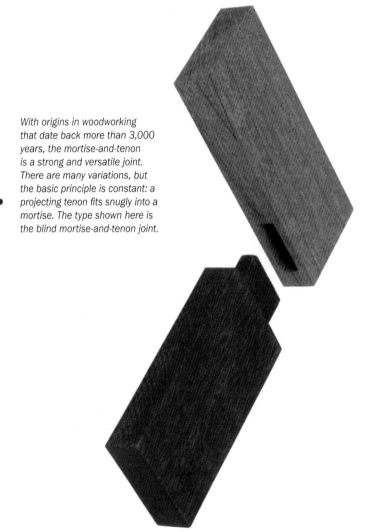

ROUTING OUT MORTISES

Using an edge guide

Use the tenon, which you can cut with a saw, to outline the mortise on the edge of the workpiece. Then secure the stock edge-up in a vise along with a support board to keep the

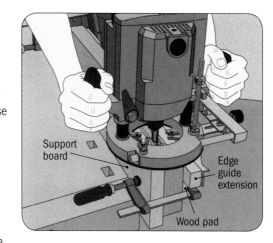

Support board

Edge guide extension

Wood pad

router steady during the cut; make certain the top surfaces of the two boards are level, and use a wood pad to protect your stock. Install a mortising bit of the same diameter as the width of the mortise, then set the depth of cut. For a deep mortise, make one or more intermediate passes. Attach a wooden extension to the fence of a commercial edge guide, then fasten the guide to the router base plate. Center the bit over the outline and adjust the extension

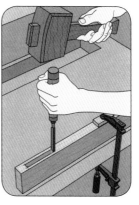

so it rests flush against the workpiece. Holding the router firmly, plunge the bit into the stock at one end of the mortise *(top)*, then feed the cutter to the other end. Once the cut is completed, clamp the stock to a work surface and square the corners of the mortise with a chisel *(bottom)*, keeping the blade square to the workpiece and the bevel facing the waste.

WORKING WITH A MORTISING SUB-BASE

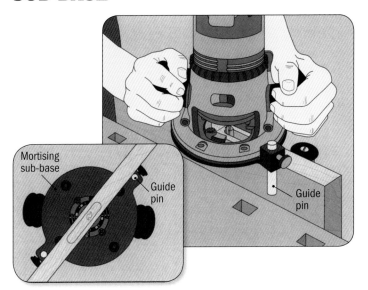

Mortising sub-base

Guide pin

Guide pin

Another way to rout mortises is to attach a commercial mortising sub-base to your router's base plate. The jig features two guide pins designed to butt against opposite faces of a workpiece *(inset)*, ensuring that the mortise is centered on the edge. Secure the stock edge-up in a vise and mark the beginning and end of the mortise. Rout the mortise as you would with an edge guide, making sure the guide pins both ride along the workpiece throughout the cut *(above)*.

ROUTING DEEP THROUGH MORTISES

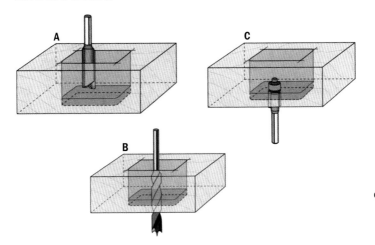

With the aid of an electric drill, your router can make mortises that exceed its maximum depth of cut. The illustration above shows the three steps necessary to cut a mortise through a thick workpiece. Start by installing a mortising bit in the router and making as many passes as you can until you can go no deeper (A). Then use the drill with a bit bigger than your router bit to bore a hole through the remaining waste (B). Install a piloted flush-trimming bit in the router and turn the workpiece over. Inserting the bit through the hole made by the drill, rout out the waste (C); keep the pilot bearing pressed against the walls of the cavity to complete the mortise.

ROUTING A MORTISE-AND-TENON

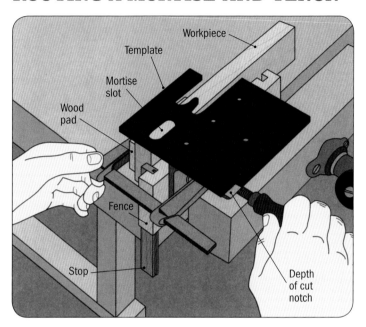

Workpiece

Template

Mortise slot

Wood pad

Fence

Stop

Depth of cut notch

Setting up the jig

Assemble a commercial mortise-and-tenon jig following the manufacturer's instructions. The model shown allows you to rout both the mortise and tenon. Secure the jig in a vise, then clamp the workpiece to it, butting the end of the board against the stop and the edge to be mortised against the template. Use wood pads to protect the stock *(above)*. Install the piloted bit supplied with the jig in your router. Use the jig's depth-of-cut notch as an aid to setting the router bit's cutting depth.

ROUTING THE MORTISE

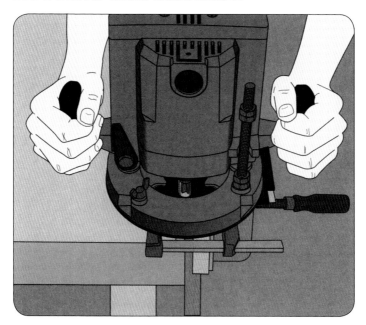

If you are using a plunge router, hold the router flat on the jig template
with the bit centered over one end of the mortise slot. Turn on the tool
and plunge the bit into the stock *(above)*. With a standard router, you
will need to angle the tool and slowly lower the bit into the workpiece.
In either case, feed the tool along the template to the other end of the
slot to finish the cut, pressing the bit pilot against the inside edge of
the slot throughout the cut. Keep the cutting edge from touching the
template at any time. Unclamp the stock from the jig and remove the jig
from the vise.

ADJUSTING THE JIG
FOR THE TENON

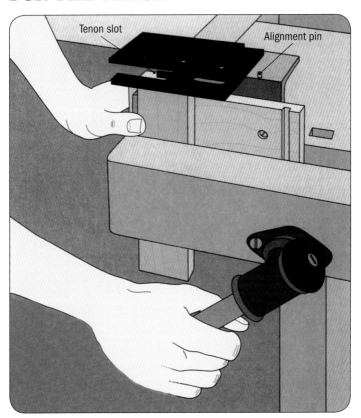

Tenon slot

Alignment pin

Remove the jig stop from the fence and fit it in the fence slot at the opposite end of the jig. Unscrew the template from the jig body and shift the template toward the tenon-end slots so that one of the alignment pins on the jig body is exposed. Refasten the template. Secure the jig and the tenon workpiece in the vise, positioning the stock so that its edge butts against the stop and its end is flush against the template *(above)*.

ROUTING THE TENON

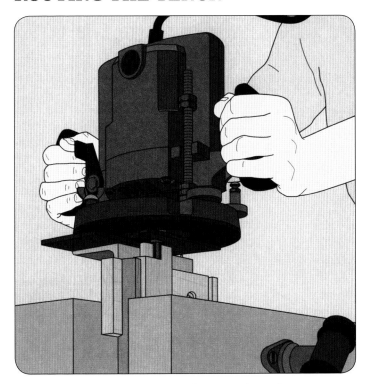

Cut the tenon in two steps. One end of the tenon is cut the same way you routed the mortise before, guiding the bit pilot along the inside edges of the tenon slots *(above)*. Then, without moving the workpiece, unscrew the template from the jig body and turn it end-for-end, keeping the same alignment pin exposed as for the first pass. Finish routing the tenon.

COPE-AND-STICK JOINTS

Used in frame-and-panel construction, the cope-and-stick joint provides strength comparable to the mortise-and-tenon while adding a decorative touch. The router bit that cuts the grooves for the panel and tongues also carves a decorative molding along the inside edges of the frame.

ROUTING A COPE-AND-STICK JOINT ON THE ROUTER TABLE

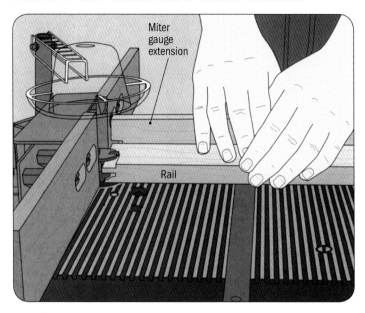

Miter gauge extension

Rail

Cutting the tongues in the rails

Make a cope-and-stick joint by first cutting tongues in the ends of both rails. Then rout grooves for the panel along the inside edges of all four frame pieces; the grooves in the stiles will accommodate the rail tongues at the same time. To cut the tongues, install a piloted coping bit—or rail cutter—in your router and mount the tool in a table. Set the cutting depth by butting the end of a rail against the bit and adjusting the router's depth setting so that the top of the uppermost cutter is slightly above the workpiece. Position the fence parallel to the miter gauge slot and in line with the edge of the bit pilot. Fit the miter gauge with an extension and press the outside face of the stock flat on the table; keep the ends of the workpiece and extension butted against the fence throughout each cut *(above)*.

ADJUSTING THE STICKING BIT

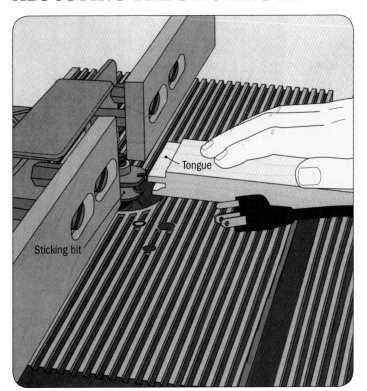

Tongue

Sticking bit

Replace the coping bit with a piloted sticking bit—also known as a stile cutter. To set the cutting depth, butt the end of a completed rail against the bit, and raise or lower the bit until one of the groove-cutting teeth is level with the rail tongue *(above)*. Align the fence with the edge of the bit pilot.

CUTTING THE GROOVES

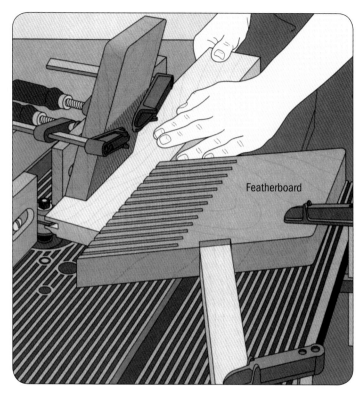

Featherboard

Use three featherboards to secure the workpiece during the cut. Clamp one to the router table opposite the bit, securing a support board at a 90° angle to the jig. Clamp the other two featherboards to the fence on either side of the cutter. (In this illustration, the featherboard on the outfeed side of the fence has been removed for clarity.) Make each cut with the stock outside-face down, pressing the workpiece against the fence *(above)*. Use a push stick to complete the pass. Repeat this groove cut on all the rails and stiles.

A MORTISING JIG

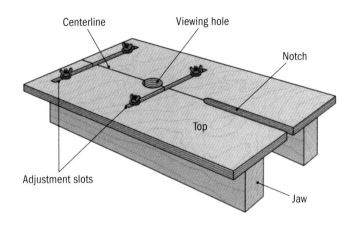

Centerline
Viewing hole
Notch
Adjustment slots
Top
Jaw

The jig above allows you to rout a mortise in stock of any thickness. Its adjustable jaws ensure that the mortise will be positioned properly, normally centered in the edge of the board.

Cut the jig top from ¾-inch plywood; make the piece about 15 inches long and wide enough to accept the thickest stock you expect to mortise. Cut the two jaws from 2-by-4-inch stock, sawing the pieces to the same length as the top. To prepare the top, mark a line down its center, then cut a notch along the line at one end using a router. The notch should be as wide as the template guide you will use with your router bit. (If you are using a top-piloted bit, rather than a non-piloted straight bit with a template guide, size the notch to accommodate the bearing.) The notch should be long enough to accommodate the longest mortise you expect to cut. Next, rout two adjustment slots perpendicular to the centerline. Finally, bore a viewing hole between the two slots. To assemble the jig, screw hanger bolts into the jaws, then fasten the top to the jaws with washers and wing nuts.

A MORTISING JIG *(continued)*

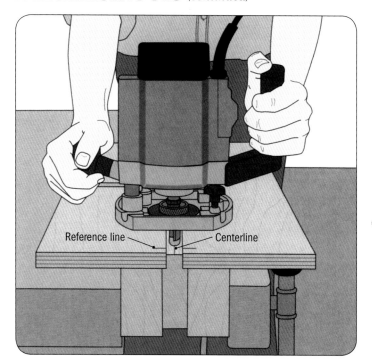

Reference line · Centerline

To use the jig, outline the mortise on the workpiece and mark a line down its center. Loosen the wing nuts and secure the stock between the jaws so the centerline is aligned with the line on the jig top; make sure the top edge of the workpiece is butted up against the top. Tighten the wing nuts. Align the bit with one end of the outline, then mark reference lines on the jig top along the edge of the router base plate. Repeat to mark lines at the other end of the outline. Rout the mortise *(above)*, starting the cut with the base plate aligned with the first set of reference lines and stopping it when the plate reaches the second set.

A TENONING JIG

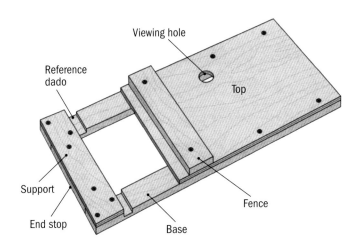

Made of solid wood and plywood, the jig shown above allows your router to cut square, two-shouldered tenons. The stock sits face-down under the jig while the router rides along a fence on top, removing waste in two passes.

The jig consists of two parallel base pieces, an end stop, and a fence—all made of wood the same thickness as the workpiece, in this case 1-by-3 stock—and a top and support made of ½-inch plywood.

The base pieces should be about 16 inches long; cut the plywood top about 8 by 10 inches and screw it to the base strips as shown at right. Screw the end stop in place underneath the support, and attach the ends of the support to the base strips. Fix the fence about 1 inch from the end of the top.

Countersink all screw heads and be sure to make all angles square. Bore a viewing hole through the top to help you position the workpiece against the base.

A TENONING JIG *(continued)*

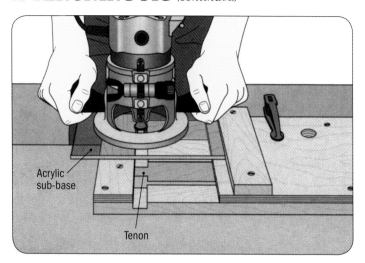

Acrylic sub-base

Tenon

You will also need to construct an acrylic sub-base for your router. It should be at least as wide as your router's base and long enough to extend from the fence beyond the end stop; a 10- or 12-inch-square piece will serve well.

Install a ¾-inch bit in the router, then remove the standard sub-base from the tool and use it as a template to mark the screw holes and bit clearance hole in the acrylic sub-base. The new sub-base must be attached to the router so that the edge of the bit lines up with the inner edge of the support and end stop when it rides along the fence. Bore the holes and attach the sub-base to the router.

To use the jig, butt the end of your workpiece against the end stop and the edge flush against the base. Clamp the assembly in place. Set the router's cutting depth and rout out the waste for half the tenon, riding the sub-base along the fence throughout the cut. (You will rout reference dadoes into the base pieces at the same time.) Turn the workpiece over and repeat the cut to complete the tenon *(above)*.

DOVETAIL JOINTS

Four dovetail joints produced with a router: *(clockwise from bottom left) dovetail spline, sliding dovetail, through dovetail,* and *half-blind dovetail. Although each joint was fashioned with the aid of a commercial jig, all possess the strength and appearance of hand-crafted joinery.*

ROUTING HALF-BLIND DOVETAILS

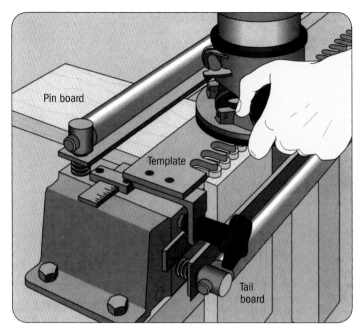

Pin board

Template

Tail board

Using an interchangeable-template jig

Set up a commercial jig for half-blind dovetails following the manufacturer's instructions. On the model shown, this involves clamping the pin and tail boards in position against the body of the jig, and securing the appropriate template atop the workpieces. Install the proper bit and template guide on your router, then rout the pins and tails in two passes: Start from the right-hand edge and make a light cut along the edge of the tail board. This will reduce tearout and ensure that all the waste around the tails will be removed. Then make a second full pass starting at the left-hand end of the workpieces, following the contours of the router's template and moving in and out of the slots *(above)*; keep the template guide flush against the edges of the fingers at all times. This will cut the pins and complete the tails simultaneously.

TWO JIGS FOR ROUTING THROUGH DOVETAILS

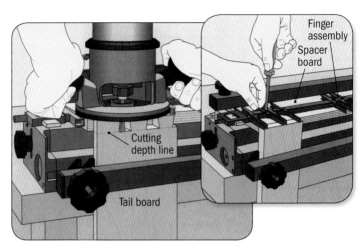

Finger assembly

Spacer board

Cutting depth line

Tail board

Using an adjustable dovetail jig

The jig shown on this page features an adjustable finger assembly that allows you to set the size of the pins and tails you rout as well as the space between them. Adjusting the assembly for the tails automatically gives you the proper size and spacing of the pins. Install a dovetail bit in your router, then set up the jig following the manufacturer's instructions. Clamp a spacer board of ¾-inch plywood to the top of the jig body, and secure the tail board outside-face out. Once the fingers are laid out over the tail board according to the size and spacing you want *(inset)*, use the thickness of the pin board as a guide to mark a cutting depth line across the tail board. Flip over the finger assembly and set the depth of cut on the router to cut the tails *(above)*.

TWO JIGS FOR ROUTING THROUGH DOVETAILS *(continued)*

Pin board

Rout from right to left, keeping the base plate flat on the fingers. To cut the pins, remove the tail board and turn over the finger assembly. Install a straight bit in the router and clamp the pin board to the jig. Mark a cutting depth line on the board, set the router's depth adjustment, and rout the pins *(above)*.

USING DOVETAIL TEMPLATES

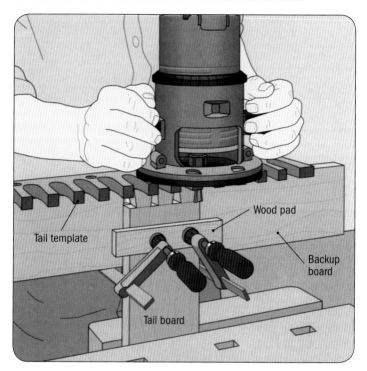

Tail template

Wood pad

Backup board

Tail board

To rout through dovetails with the dovetail templates shown on this page, attach the pin and tail templates to backup boards following the manufacturer's instructions. Secure the tail board in a vise end-up and clamp the backup board to it, making sure there will be half-tails at both edges; the template and backup board should be flush against the workpiece. Protect the stock with a wood pad. If you are cutting several workpieces, butt a stop block against the first workpiece and clamp the block to the backup board. Install the dovetail bit and template guide supplied with the jig and cut the tails, feeding the tool in and out of the template slots *(above)*. Unclamp the tail board from

USING DOVETAIL TEMPLATES *(continued)*

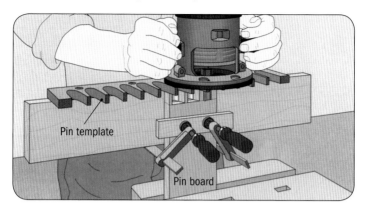

Pin template

Pin board

the vise and use it to outline the pins on the pin board. Secure the pin board in the vise and clamp the pin template to the stock, aligning the jig fingers with the marked outline. Remove the dovetail bit from the router, install the straight bit supplied with the jig, and rout out the waste between the pins *(above)*.

MAKING A SLIDING DOVETAIL JOINT

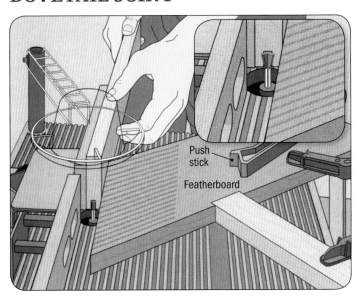

Push stick

Featherboard

Cutting the dovetail groove

Cut the dovetail groove in two passes on a router table. For the first pass, install a straight bit. Adjust the depth of cut, and position the fence so that the work is centered over the bit. Clamp a featherboard to the table to secure the workpiece during the cut; to apply extra pressure, clamp a support board at a 90° angle to the featherboard. Feed the workpiece into the bit with both hands *(above)*, pressing the stock flat against the fence throughout the cut. Finish the cut with a push stick. For the second pass, install a dovetail bit *(inset)* and complete the groove by feeding the workpiece into the bit while pressing the stock tightly against the fence.

CUTTING THE DOVETAIL SLIDE

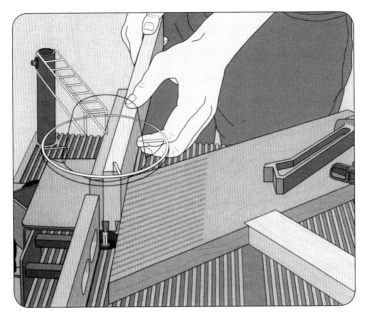

With the dovetail bit still in the router, shift the fence toward the bit so that half the diameter of the cutter projects beyond the fence. Reposition the featherboard. Reduce the cutting depth slightly so that the slide is not as deep as the groove; this will improve the fit of the joint. Cut the slide in two passes, removing the waste from one side at a time *(above)*. Test-fit the joint and readjust the position of the fence if it is necessary to trim the slide.

A JIG FOR SLIDING DOVETAILS

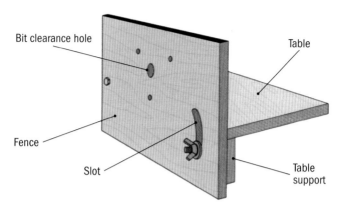

The jig shown above allows you to rout sliding dovetails without a router table. The device features a fence that holds the router and a pivoting adjustable table for aligning the workpiece with the bit. Cut the fence, table, and support piece from ¾-inch plywood. Make all the boards 16 inches long; the fence and table should be about 10 inches wide and the support piece about 3 inches wide. Screw the table to the support piece so they form an L shape. Position the table 4 inches from the top of the fence and bore two holes through the fence into the table support. With a straight bit in a router, lengthen the hole on the outfeed side of the fence into a curved slot. Fasten the adjustable end of the table support to the fence with a carriage bolt, washer, and a wing nut. Bolt the infeed side just loose enough for the table to be able to pivot when the other end is raised or lowered.

To prepare the fence for your router, remove the sub-base and use it as a template to mark the screw holes and bit clearance hole on the fence. The bottom edge of the clearance hole should line up with the top of the jig table when the table is level; in the illustration above, the table is in the lowest position.

A JIG FOR SLIDING DOVETAILS *(continued)*

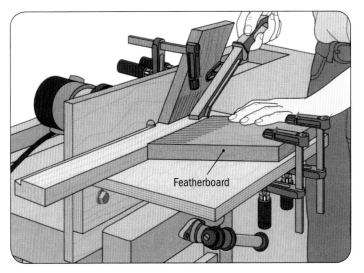

Featherboard

To use the jig, secure the fence in a vise and rout the dovetail groove first, then the matching slide. For the groove, install a bit in the router, attach the tool to the jig fence, and adjust the cutting depth. Set the workpiece face-down on the table, butting its edge against the bit. Loosen the wing nut and adjust the table to center the bit on the edge of the stock, then tighten the nut. Secure the workpiece with three featherboards: Clamp one to the table in line with the bit and the other two to the fence on both sides of the cutter. (In the illustration, the featherboard on the outfeed side of the fence has been removed for clarity.) Rout the groove as you would on a router table, using first a straight bit, then a dovetail bit *(page 170)*. To cut the slide, set your workpiece on the table and lower the table to produce a ⅛-inch-wide cut. Make a pass on each side, finishing the cut with a push stick *(above)*. Test-fit the joint; if necessary, raise the table slightly and make another pass on each side of the stock.

ROUTING A DOVETAIL SPLINE JOINT

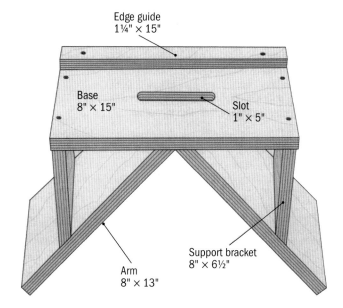

Edge guide
1¼" × 15"

Base
8" × 15"

Slot
1" × 5"

Arm
8" × 13"

Support bracket
8" × 6½"

Making the jig

The jig shown above, built from ¾-inch plywood, will help you cut grooves for dovetail spline joints in the corners of a carcase. Refer to the illustration for suggested dimensions. Before assembling the jig, cut the oval slot in the middle of the base to accommodate your bit. Cut 45° bevels at the top ends of the arms and the bottom ends of the support brackets. Attach the arms to the base and the brackets to the base and arms, making the arms perpendicular to each other and centering them under the slot. Install a dovetail bit in your router, secure the jig in a vise and, with the bit in the slot, position the edge guide against the tool's base plate and screw it down. Then, with the base plate pressed against the guide, rout a channel across the top ends of the arms.

ROUTING THE GROOVES

Wood pad

Carcase

Mark cutting lines for the grooves on the corners of the workpiece. Secure the carcase diagonally in a vise and set the jig on top, aligning the edges of the channel you routed before with one of the cutting marks. Clamp the jig to the carcase, protecting the stock with wood pads. Rout the grooves by repeating the cut you made to rout the channel, feeding the bit through the corner of the carcase. Be sure to keep the router flat on the jig base and flush against the edge guide until the bit is well clear of the carcase. Reposition the jig and repeat to rout the other grooves *(above)*.

INSERTING THE SPLINES

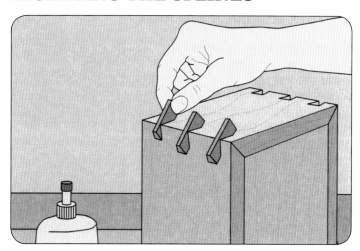

To make enough splines for several grooves, rout a dovetail slide on the edge of a board, just as you would for a sliding dovetail joint *(page 170)*. Rip the slide from the board on a table saw, then cut individual splines from it. For a snug fit, use the same dovetail bit that cut the grooves before. Install the splines by spreading some glue in the grooves and on the splines and sliding them in place *(above)*. Once the glue has dried, trim off excess wood with a handsaw and sand the surface flush with the carcase.

A ROUTER-TABLE JIG

The jig shown at right allows you to rout a series of evenly spaced grooves for straight or dovetail splines. Cut a V-shaped notch into the face of a board, then install a ¼-inch straight bit in your router and mount the tool in a table. Screw the jig to a miter gauge and feed it into the bit to make a notch. Fit and glue a wood key in the notch, then reposition the jig on the gauge so the distance

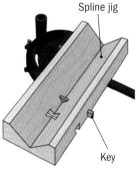

Spline jig

Key

between the key and the bit equals the spacing you want between the spline grooves. Feed the jig into the bit to rout a second notch. Install a ½-inch dovetail bit and set the depth of cut so the full dovetail shape is visible above the bottom of the notch. To use the jig, seat the workpiece in the V with an edge butted against the key and rout the first groove. To cut subsequent grooves, fit the groove over the key and slide the workpiece into the bit *(above top)*.

CUTTING A GLUE JOINT ON A ROUTER TABLE

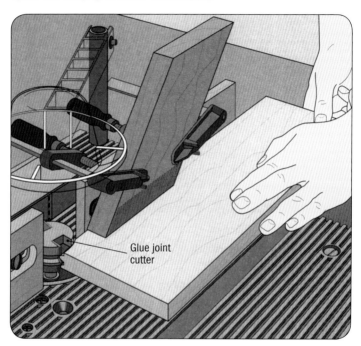

Glue joint cutter

Making the cuts

Install a glue joint cutter in your router, mount the tool in a table and set the cutting depth. Secure the workpiece with two featherboards clamped to the fence on either side of the bit. (In the illustration, the featherboard on the outfeed side of the fence has been removed for clarity.) Before you cut the joint, make test cuts in two scrap boards. Flip one board over, test-fit the joint and, if necessary, adjust the depth of cut until the mated surfaces of the two boards are flush. To make a pass, feed the stock into the bit with your right hand while keeping it pressed firmly against the fence with your left hand *(above)*.

GLUE JOINTS

Used to reinforce glued-up panels, the glue joint consists of two boards with identical cuts in their edges. Both cuts are produced on a router table with the same bit; one of the boards is flipped to mate with the other.

ROUTING A BOX JOINT

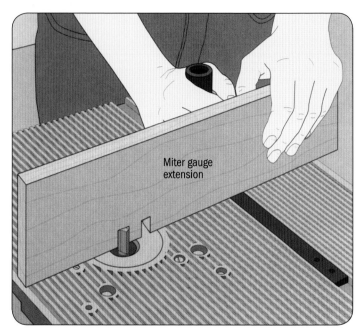

Miter gauge
extension

Setting up the jig

The jig shown above allows you to cut the notches for a box joint one at
a time on a router table. The jig is simply an extension board screwed
to the miter gauge and fitted with a key to determine the spacing of the
notches. Install a straight bit with the same diameter as the desired
width of the notches; mount the router in a table. Set the depth of cut
to equal the thickness of your stock and feed the extension into the bit
to rout a notch. Then unscrew the extension from the miter gauge and
reposition it so that the gap between the notch and the bit equals the
width of the bit. Feed the extension into the bit again, cutting a second
notch *(above)*. Fashion a wood key to fit in the first notch and glue it in
place so it projects about 1 inch from the extension board.

BOX JOINTS

The box joint, also known as a finger joint, is ideal for making drawers or cabinets. The joint derives its strength from the large gluing area of the interlocking pins and notches.

CUTTING THE NOTCHES IN THE FIRST BOARD

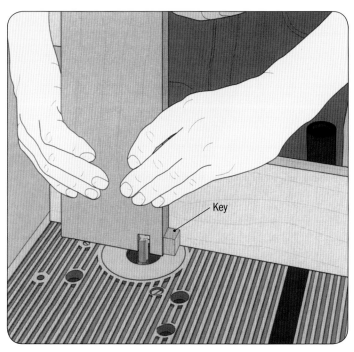

Key

Holding the face of the workpiece against the miter gauge extension, butt one edge against the key. Turn on the router and, hooking your thumbs around the gauge, slide the board into the bit, cutting the first notch *(above)*. Fit the notch over the key and make a second cut. Continue cutting notches this way until you reach the opposite edge of the workpiece.

CUTTING THE NOTCHES
IN THE MATING BOARD

Mating board

Fit the last notch of the first board over the key. Butt one edge of the mating board against the first board, and move the entire assembly forward to cut the first notch in the mating board; hold both pieces flush against the miter gauge extension *(above)*. Cut the remaining notches in the mating board by following the same procedure used for the first board.

MITER-AND-SPLINE JOINTS

The miter-and-spline is essentially a simple miter joint with a spline glued into grooves cut in mitered ends; it is often used in frame-and-panel construction. The spline is either plywood or solid wood with grain that runs perpendicular to the miter cuts.

TWO WAYS OF ROUTING A MITER-AND-SPLINE JOINT

Using a straight bit

Make 45° miter cuts in each workpiece. Install a straight bit in your router and mount the tool in a table. Set the cutting depth so the groove you cut will accommodate one-half the width of your spline. To secure the workpiece, clamp a featherboard to the table in line with the bit. Rest the featherboard on a shim so the stock will be held flat against the fence; clamp a support board at a 90° angle to the featherboard to apply extra pressure. Rout the spline grooves by feeding the workpiece on end into the bit, keeping its face flush against the fence *(above)*. Once all the grooves have been made, cut a spline for each joint; make it twice as wide as the groove depth, less ¹⁄₃₂ inch for clearance. For maximum strength, use plywood or solid wood with the grain running across the width of the spline, rather than lengthwise.

TWO WAYS OF ROUTING A MITER-AND-SPLINE JOINT *(continued)*

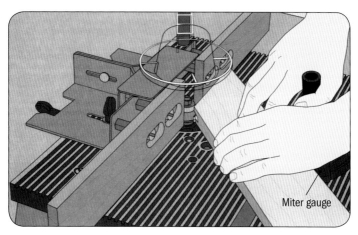

Miter gauge

Using a Three-Wing Slotting Cutter

You can also rout the grooves for miter-and-spline joints by using a three-wing slotting cutter and feeding the stock face-down into the bit. Position the fence in line with the bit pilot, making the cutting width equal to one-half the bit diameter. To set the depth of cut, place the workpiece flat on the table and center the bit's tooth on the edge of the stock. Feed the workpiece into the cutter with a miter gauge, holding the edge of the board flush against the gauge and one mitered end flat along the fence *(above)*.

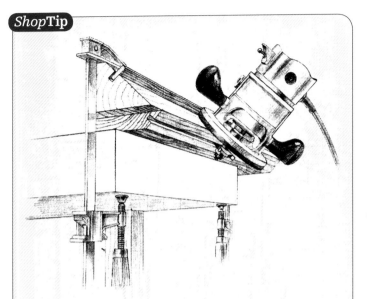

A miter-and-spline jig

To rout the groove for a miter-and-spline joint along a board edge, use
the jig shown here. Cut a 4-by-4 longer than your workpiece, then rip it
diagonally. In one piece, joint the cut surface, rout a groove down its middle,
and glue a spline in the groove to serve as an edge guide. To use the jig, cut
a 45° bevel along the edge of the workpiece, then clamp the stock and the
jig to a table with the edge of the workpiece slightly overhanging the jig. Use
the router fitted with a straight bit to trim the beveled edge, then install a
three-wing slotting cutter and repeat to rout the groove, keeping the bit pilot
against the stock.

CUTTING A TONGUE-AND-GROOVE JOINT

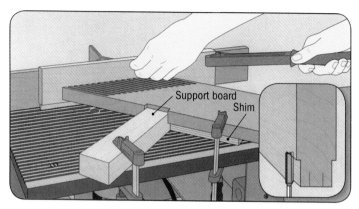

Support board
Shim

Routing the groove and tongue

Fit your router with a straight bit. Start by cutting the groove, then cut the tongue in several passes, removing the waste a little at a time *(inset)*. The tongue's depth should be slightly less than the groove. To support the workpiece during the cut, clamp a featherboard to the table and rest it on a shim so that it presses against the workpiece above the bit; clamp a support board at a 90° angle to the featherboard for extra pressure. Slowly feed the stock into the cutter. Turn the workpiece end-for-end and repeat the procedure. Finish each pass with a push stick *(above)*. Move the fence back from the bit to remove more waste and make two more passes, test-fitting the joint and continuing until the tongue fits snugly in the groove.

TONGUE-AND-GROOVE JOINTS

With its long gluing surface, the tongue-and-groove joint is commonly used to strengthen carcase joinery and to assemble glued-up panels and solid cabinet doors.

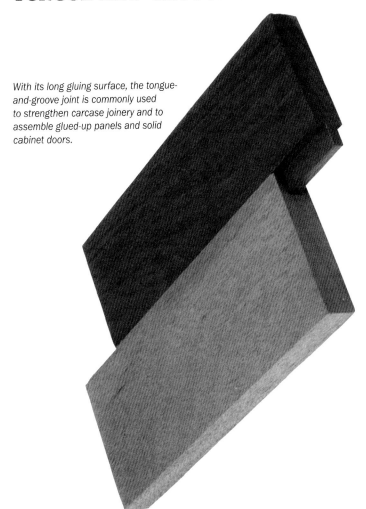

RULE JOINTS

A common feature of drop-leaf tables, the rule joint consists of two matching hinged pieces. The leaf has a cove cut along its edge that mates with the tabletop's rounded-over edge. When the leaf is down, the decorative edge is visible.

MAKING A RULE JOINT

Making the cut in the tabletop

Clamp the tabletop to a work surface with the edge to be shaped extending off the surface. Install a piloted round-over bit and adjust the cutting depth to allow you to

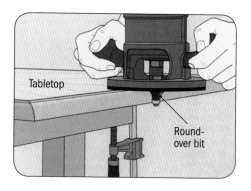

Tabletop

Round-over bit

reach the final depth in at least two passes. As you make the cut, press the bit pilot against the stock throughout the pass *(above)*. For a smooth finish, make your final pass a slow and shallow one.

SHAPING THE LEAF
AND INSTALLING THE HINGE

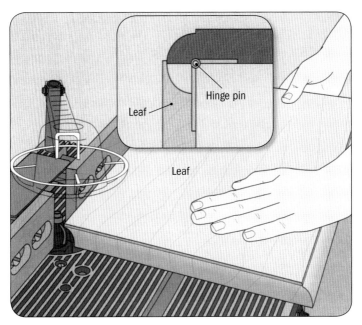

Hinge pin

Leaf

Leaf

Install a piloted cove bit whose diameter and profile match the one used before, then mount the router in a table. Align the fence with the bit pilot so that the width of cut will equal one-half the cutter diameter. Set the depth of cut to reach your final depth in several passes. Feed the leaf into the bit, bracing its edge against the fence *(above)*. After each pass, test-fit the pieces; continue cutting until the tabletop and leaf mesh with a slight gap between the two. Finish the joint by installing a rule-joint hinge on the undersides of the pieces: Position one hinge leaf against the tabletop and the other against the leaf so the hinge pin is aligned with the start of the round-over cut on the tabletop *(inset)*. Outline and then rout mortises for the hinge leaves in the tabletop and the leaf. Screw the hinge in place.

CHAPTER 5:
Freehand Routing

Freehand cutting with a router, guiding the tool only with steady eyes and hands, is similar to sculpture, requiring practice and patience. Although experience will help you settle on the wood species, methods, and types of bits that work best for you, even a novice can achieve satisfactory results—provided the routing is done with care.

Freehand routing will allow you to do relief cutting, which involves carving away the waste surrounding the pattern you want, leaving the raised form on the surface, as shown in the photo at right. You can also do incised cutting (page 199), in which the waste sections are the final product.

Until you become comfortable with the techniques of freehand routing, practice on scrap wood—and heed the suggestions and tips presented on page 195. The remaining pages of this section show how freehand routing can cut relief and incised lettering.

Fitted with a clear acrylic sub-base and a ¼-inch veining bit, a router is used freehand to carve lettering into a piece of wood. The sub-base is transparent so the user can view the cutting action, and it is wider than a standard sub-base to help keep the router steady on the workpiece.

FREEHAND ROUTER BITS

Veining bit

Straight bit

Cove bit

V-groove bit

Lettering bit

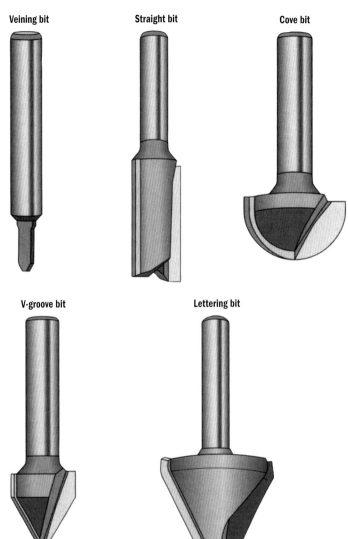

PRINCIPLES OF FREEHAND ROUTING

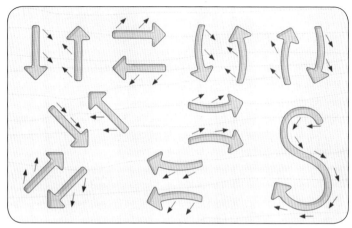

Illustration courtesy of Patrick Spielman

Guiding a router in freehand cutting

The large arrows in silhouette form in the illustration above represent several commonly used freehand router strokes, ranging from straight and diagonal cuts to gentle arcs and long, sinuous curves. The red arrows indicate the direction in which the router will tend to move as you make these cuts. To obtain the cut you want, you will have to counterbalance this tendency with feed pressure. With experience, applying the right amount of pressure in the proper direction will become second nature. For best results, always pull the router toward you, rather than pushing the tool into a cut. For deep cuts, it is best to make several intermediate passes. To minimize splintering, cut from waste sections toward uncut wood instead of the other way around. And avoid back strain by setting up your work at a comfortable height—which for most people is at the level of the base of the spine.

SAFETY TIPS

- Only use well-sharpened bits, and preferably ones that feature an anti-kickback design.

- Wear eye and ear protection.

- Avoid working when you are tired or under the influence of alcohol or medication.

- Make several shallow passes to complete a cut, rather than one deep cut.

- Apply adequate pressure to counter the router's pulling tendency.

- Install the bit in the router so that at least three-quarters of the shaft is in the collet.

- Hook up your router to a dust collection system.

- To avoid sudden distractions, keep pets, children, and onlookers away while you are working.

- Unplug your router whenever you are changing bits.

RELIEF CARVING WITH
THE ROUTER

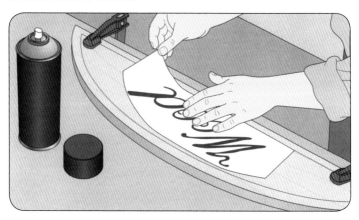

Transferring the pattern

Sketch or photocopy your pattern on a piece of paper and affix it to the
workpiece *(above)*. If you use a spray adhesive, you will be able to peel
the pattern off the surface when the carving is completed.

MAKING AND INSTALLING
AN ACRYLIC ROUTER SUB-BASE

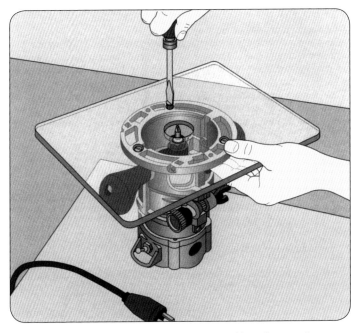

Replace the standard sub-base on your router with a clear acrylic one; this will enable you to view the cutting action as you rout the pattern. Cut the sub-base from ¼- or ⅜-inch-thick acrylic plastic, making the piece as large as necessary to keep the router steady on the workpiece; as a rule of thumb, the sub-base should be twice as wide as the workpiece. Use your standard sub-base as a template for drilling the bit clearance and screw holes through the acrylic, then fasten the sub-base to the router *(above)*.

DEFINING THE PATTERN

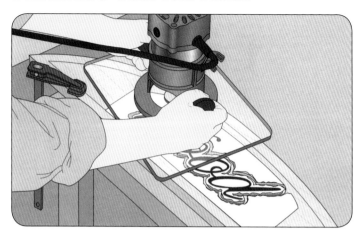

Install a small-diameter bit in your router; the cutter in the illustrations on this page is a ¼-inch veining bit. Starting at one end of the pattern, cut along its edges to remove the waste just outside the marked lines. Work on the outside edges of the pattern, then move on to the waste areas on the inside edges. Keep the sub-base flat on the workpiece throughout the operation *(above)*, guiding the router against the direction of bit rotation whenever possible.

ROUTING OUT THE REMAINING WASTE

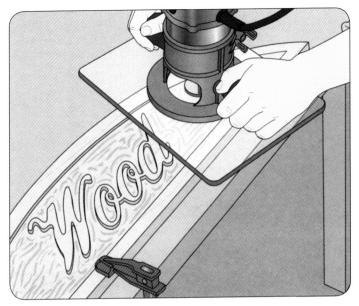

Feed the router in a series of back-and-forth, side-to-side passes to clear the waste remaining around the pattern. By varying the router's feed direction, you can impart a hand-carved texture to the workpiece *(above)*. Use a chisel, if necessary, to remove waste from tight spots.

ROUTING SERIF LETTERS

Guide
line

Outlining the letter patterns

Clamp your stock to a work surface and mark two parallel lines along
the surface, spaced to equal the desired height of your letters. Then
use a pencil to outline the letters on the surface. You can either sketch
the letters freehand *(above)* or trace them from a pattern; for an
elegant, traditional look, you can reproduce the Old English letters
shown at right. Try to match the width of the letters' strokes to the
diameter of the bit you will be using. To produce a traceable pattern
of the appropriate size, use a photocopier with an enlargement feature;
then, secure the finished pattern to the workpiece.

AN ALPHABET OF OLD ENGLISH-STYLE SERIF LETTERS

MAKING THE STRAIGHT CUTS

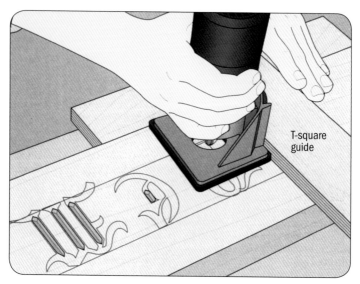

T-square
guide

Install a 60° V- bit in a laminate trimmer, set a shallow cutting depth, and start by routing the letters' straight elements; leave the serifs, or tail-like strokes on the top and bottom ends of the letters, for later. Use a T-square jig to guide each cut; align the bit with the outline and butt the arm of the jig against the edge of the workpiece with the fence on the top surface and flush against the trimmer's base plate. Holding the jig in place, turn on the tool, plunge the bit into the stock at the beginning of the straight portion, and cut along it, pulling the trimmer toward you. Hold the base plate flat on the workpiece and flush against the edge guide throughout *(above)*.

ROUTING THE SERIFS

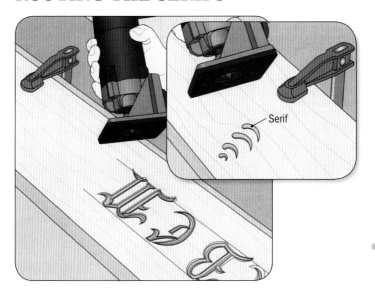

Before adding the serifs to the letters, practice making the curved cuts in a piece of scrap wood *(inset)*. Cut the serifs by starting at their deeper, wider ends. Plunge the bit into the stock, rout the pattern, and slowly withdraw the bit from the wood while feeding the tool along the surface; this action will produce the narrow tail of the serif. Once you are satisfied with your serif-making abilities, add this detail to your letters *(above)*.

Index

Index

INDEX

Back to **Basics**

Straight Talk for Today's **Woodworker**

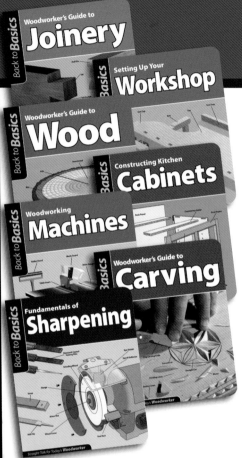

Woodworker's Guide to Joinery
ISBN 978-1-56523-462-8
$19.95 • 192 Pages

Setting Up Your Workshop
ISBN 978-1-56523-463-5
$19.95 • 152 Pages

Woodworker's Guide to Wood
ISBN 978-1-56523-464-2
$19.95 • 160 Pages

Constructing Kitchen Cabinets
ISBN 978-1-56523-466-6
$19.95 • 144 Pages

Woodworking Machines
ISBN 978-1-56523-465-9
$19.95 • 192 Pages

Woodworker's Guide to Carving
ISBN 978-1-56523-497-0
$19.95 • 160 Pages

Fundamentals of Sharpening
Coming Winter 2011

Get *Back to Basics* with the core information you need to succeed. This new series offers a clear road map of fundamental woodworking knowledge on sixteen essential topics. It explains what's important to know now and what can be left for later. Best of all, it's presented in the plain-spoken language you'd hear from a trusted friend or relative. The world's already complicated—your woodworking shouldn't be.

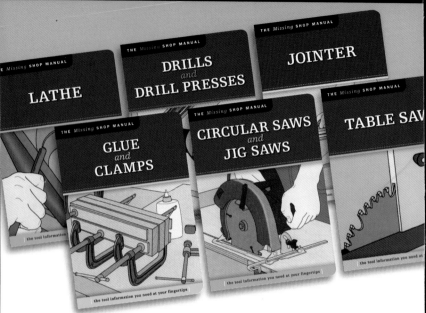